What Every

M♥m
Needs

Meet *Your* Nine Basic Needs
(and Be a Better Mom)

What Every

M♥m
Needs

MOTHERS OF
M♥PS.
PRESCHOOLERS

Elisa Morgan &
Carol Kuykendall

ZondervanPublishingHouse
Grand Rapids, Michigan

A Division of HarperCollinsPublishers

What Every Mom Needs
Copyright © 1995 by MOPS International, Inc.

Requests for information should be addressed to:

Zondervan Publishing House
Grand Rapids, Michigan 49530

Library of Congress Cataloging-in-Publication Data

Morgan, Elisa, 1955–
    What every mom needs: meet your nine basic needs (and be a better mom) /
Elisa Morgan and Carol Kuykendall.
       p.   cm.
    Includes bibliographical references.
    ISBN: 0–310–20097–0 (hardcover : acid-free paper)
    1. Mothers—Psychology. 2. Mothers—Life skills guides. 3. Mothers—
Religious life. I. Kuykendall, Carol, 1945– . II. Title.
HQ759.M863. 1995
646.7'0085'2—dc 20
                                95–12700
                                    CIP

This edition printed on acid-free paper and meets the American National Standards
Institute Z39.48 standard.

Edited by Mary McCormick
Interior design by Sherri L. Hoffman

*At the time of publication, MOPS International was represented by Alive
Communications, Inc., Colorado Springs, CO 80949.*

Printed in the United States of America

---

95 96 97 98 99 00 / ❖ DH / 10 9 8 7 6 5 4 3 2 1

Dedication
To every mom, with love.
You matter!

Mom, what do you need most?

— ❧ —

A sanity check.

To know that I'm normal.

To know that I'm a good mother.

Acceptance.

Encouragement.

Support.

Time.

Time with my husband.

Time off.

Time alone.

Time with God.

Patience.

More energy.

A break.

A nap.

A housekeeper.

A secretary.

A nanny.

*A dishwasher that loads itself and a vacuum that runs by
remote control.*

A vacation.

Adult conversation.

Friends.

A best friend.

Someone to understand how I feel.

To know that being a mother is important.

Contents

Acknowledgments

This book represents twenty-two years of work by women and men associated with MOPS International. It is their faithful vision of reaching every mother of preschoolers that has kept MOPS vibrant and effective. Specifically, we would like to thank:

— the moms who have participated in MOPS since 1973
— the board of MOPS International, both past and present
— the moms who responded to one thousand questionnaires sent out and tabulated for use in this book
— the staff of MOPS International with special recognition given to:

Kaye Burich
Kelli Gourley
Michele Hall
Marcy Naumann
Karen Parks

Thanks for keeping MOPS in your heart!

Further, we are also grateful for the partnership of Zondervan Publishing House and the input of Scott Bolinder and Sandy Vander Zicht. Thanks for making it more possible for us to reach "every mom."

And to Rick Christian, many thanks for helping our voice be heard, on behalf of every mom of preschoolers.

Introduction

"I should have known that going to the grocery store wouldn't work today," Linda scolded herself as she placed two-month-old Jason into the infant seat in the cart. Already, he was fussing, and she felt embarrassed and guilty as he whimpered all the way through the produce section.

She checked her watch. Almost 2:30. No wonder he was fussy. He should be home in his crib asleep. Yet, in between feedings and quick naps, it had taken her all day until now simply to get the baby ready to go to the store.

What was wrong with her? Since becoming a mother, she'd totally lost control of her time. She used to be able to make a list and accomplish tasks efficiently. When she was pregnant, she'd pictured herself getting everything done and still having time for herself. Now she could barely get out of the house to run a single errand—like going to the grocery store—which, if she could pull it off, would probably turn out to be her one accomplishment of the day. Big whoop!

Maybe, if she cut her list in half and only bought milk and diapers and something for dinner, she could finish quickly, she decided as she headed for the frozen food section. What else was on her list? Oh, no, the list! She rummaged frantically through her purse. She must've left it at home on the kitchen counter. She sighed and pushed the cart faster.

The store seemed crowded for this time of day and, by the time she got to the dairy products, Jason had worked his fussing into pitiful wails.

By now he was bawling. Everyone within thirty feet was watching as she tried to comfort him—with no success. She finally made it through the checkout line, wheeled her groceries and Jason to the car, strapped him in, and drove home with one hand, using the other to stroke his face. He finally calmed down and, a few blocks from home, she faced another problem. Exhausted from the outing, he was about to fall asleep.

Oh, no! She needed to get him home, feed him, and put him down for a real nap so she would have time to unload and put away the groceries and think about dinner before he woke up again. She shook a rattle in his face while loudly singing his name until they pulled up in front of the house.

Quickly, Linda unbuckled herself and then Jason, slung the diaper bag and purse over her shoulder, and then heaved the infant seat up in front of her. She resisted the urge to grab a sack of groceries as well and trudged up the steps.

Once inside, she dumped her load on the table and whisked the baby to the bedroom, where she changed his diaper. Rocking him while he ate, she tried to enjoy the moment. This was the image she had envisioned when she dreamed about becoming a mother—soft moments like this, holding a serene, sweet child, the whole focus of her life.

But now thoughts of melting groceries and making dinner and doing more laundry blocked any feelings of serenity. Tears suddenly formed under her closed, heavy eyelids. She felt so tired. More tired and discouraged and alone than ever before in her whole life. She thought she could handle—even enjoy— being a mom. She thought she'd know how to do it. But this wasn't what she'd expected. This was, well, it was so *hard!*

What's the matter with me? Linda wondered.

EXPECTATIONS VERSUS REALITY

Most likely, you've been where Linda was. Maybe, for you, it was last month. Maybe it was last week. Maybe it was an hour ago. Whenever it was, this disappointment, confusion, sense of inadequacy is surprising. Mothering isn't supposed to be this way!

In the days prior to actually becoming mothers, we fantasize about motherhood, imagining it to be magical, swathed in perfect pastel images. Then reality hits.

My dreams and expectations were along the lines of a Pampers commercial—lots of smiles and coos and a perfectly happy and contented baby. Sure, there would be difficult times, but they would not get me down for long. And my love for my baby would overcome any lack of sleep or missed lunches with my girlfriends. Not so, I've learned.

And a second dreamed,

I thought my child and I would be perfect together. I pictured myself with unending energy, looking great when my husband came home. We'd sit down to a well-balanced meal, followed by family strolls in the park and quiet romantic evenings while baby slept. What a joke!

Ha! Only a few months into mothering, we face the disappointment of the gap between our expectations and the rock-hard reality of being on duty twenty-four hours a day, engaged in some of the most unseemly aspects of life.

Yes, of course there are wonderful, tender moments. Even whole hours of bliss! Caressing petal-soft skin. Fingering perfect miniature hands, dimpled at the knuckles. Smooching under chins, behind ears, and smack-dab in the center of plump cheeks. Staring deeply into eyes enraptured by our mere presence. Leaning down in response to raised-arm requests for "Uppie!" Yes, there are wondrous times in mothering!

And there are also shocking, unexpected days and weeks, when we quickly come to the end of who we are and what we know and we wonder how we're going to make it through the next twenty years . . . or twenty minutes.

MOMS HAVE NEEDS TOO!

As mothers of preschoolers, those who have children from infancy to school age, we find a widening gap between our unrealistic expectations and the undeniable reality of our day-to-day lives. And in this gap grows some of our most insistent, basic needs. Yet because of the demanding, hectic nature of our days, we don't often examine those needs, much less take time to meet them. But take a look at *this* truth: Just because we've become moms doesn't mean we're finished being children. Or students. Or pilgrims. Moms have continuing needs too. To sleep. To grow. To talk with someone who cares. To regain perspective and find hope. Ignoring those needs not only jeopardizes the health and well-being of the mom but of the whole family.

This book is about what moms need. We make two main points:

1. *Moms have needs.* They are an undeniable part of our lives and foundational to our development. As we begin to discuss them in specific, it's important that we understand them in general.

— Needs are normal. Every human being has them. Psychologists and social scientists and religious experts agree that all normal people have needs and healthy people recognize these needs. A mom who believes that she has no important needs is sure to end up feeling frustrated and empty. Needs are normal at this stage of life, as in every stage of life.

— Needs are personal. Some of your needs will be greater than others. Your needs may differ from those of your best friend. In some moments, one need may seem much greater than another and then they may trade places in importance in the very next hour.

— Needs must be recognized. Needs are nagging and insistent. They don't like to be ignored. If they don't receive the attention they demand in a healthy manner, they're apt to rear their heads in undesirable behavior. Psychologist Dr. Larry Crabb reports, "Most psychological symptoms (anxiety, depression, uncontrolled temper, pathological lying, sexual problems, irrational fears, manic highs) are either the direct result of or defensive attempts to cope with unmet personal needs."[1] However, recognizing and meeting our needs leads to positive development through this stage of life.

2. *Moms must learn to recognize and meet their own needs in order to better meet the needs of their children.* Sitting through preflight instructions on an airplane, you are told that if the oxygen masks drop down during flight and you are flying with a small child, you should first affix the oxygen mask to your own face and then assist the child. The implication is obvious: You can't help a child to breathe if you've fainted from your own lack of oxygen!

Similarly, moms cannot effectively meet the needs of their children while ignoring their own. And during the days of mothering young children with intense needs, moms must recognize the value of understanding and meeting their own needs, for the sake of their children and families.

NINE NEEDS

Nine needs are unique to the stage of life in which we are mothering children from infancy to kindergarten age. When we learn to recognize these needs in ourselves, they become the building blocks that bridge the distance between expectations and reality. If these needs are ignored, however, they become stumbling blocks, slowing our development and blocking our fulfillment as mothers.

How do we know? Because we speak for an organization— MOPS International—that has been involved in meeting the needs of mothers of preschoolers since 1973 in every state of the United States and in ten other countries. The compilation of these nine needs has come through years of research, interviews, and experience with mothers of preschoolers. In preparation for writing this book, we sent over one thousand questionnaires to moms who responded with descriptions of their needs, which are shared throughout this book.

These nine chapters were written to help moms of preschoolers both understand and meet these nine needs. Each chapter follows a basic format, beginning with a story adapted from the real-life experiences of mothers of preschoolers. The body of each chapter then discusses the need, centering on why meeting this need is so vital to the mother of preschoolers. At the end of each chapter, we've included a section of helps entitled "Building Blocks." Here is inspiration, some questions for you to answer, and a few practical suggestions for taking steps to meet this need in your life.

The entire book, including this introduction, is punctuated with the comments of mothers of preschoolers. You'll notice that when a mom speaks, we have not introduced her or identified her. Instead, her voice is set apart in italics. It is our hope that you will make friends with the women in these pages. Perhaps you will recognize someone you know, possibly even yourself.

You'll also notice that this book is written to "every" mother of preschoolers—whoever you might be and wherever you might live. Whether you work full-time inside the home or are employed outside as well. Whether you are married or single. Whatever your heritage or faith. No matter your past or your present. Whether you have three children or one. Whether you are nineteen or forty-two. This book is for you because these nine needs describe you.

Further, we believe that this book will help you make sense of what you're going through and assure you that you're not alone. You will find encouragement in its pages. And hope.

This is our hope,
Elisa Morgan
and
Carol Kuykendall
for MOPS International

What surprised you about becoming a mother?

— ❧ —

Myself.

My temper and impatience.

How tired I feel.

How much I love my child.

That a baby can take up my whole day.

That while I love my children, some days I don't like them.

How being a mom brings out the best and worst in me.

Some things I say to my children that I vowed I'd never say.

That I'll never be able to use the bathroom alone again.

How many times a nose needs to be wiped.

That a two-year-old can bring an adult to her knees in prayer faster than anything else.

That I can't punch out at five o'clock or ten o'clock or two o'clock!

How much I started worrying about germs and cigarette smoke and strangers and car accidents and . . .

That I truly understand my mother for the first time.

That I could love a second child . . . then a third . . . as much as my first.

How wonderful it is to be called "Mommy."

Significance:

Sometimes I wonder if mothering matters

Joanie padded from the refrigerator back to the couch where her recently newborn daughter lay, wrapped in a blanket. *So tiny!* Joanie thought as she scooped up the baby and cuddled her closely. But so much bigger than just two months before when the doctor had plopped her on Joanie's stomach in the delivery room. That was a moment she'd never forget.

Joanie touched Marcy's cheek tenderly and then lifted her above her head in a playful mood. "I love you, dear child, more than I ever imagined."

She continued to nuzzle the baby until she heard the familiar theme song of a television newscast. *Five o'clock!? Where did the day go? I'm not even dressed!* she thought, glancing down at her wrinkled flannel nightgown. *I've accomplished absolutely nothing today. And I used to be so organized and efficient.*

Joanie held her baby and thought back over the past several months. As a dental hygienist she'd taken more than the usual number of jokes as her tummy swelled and she awkwardly positioned herself to care for her patients. Actually, she loved her job! So many new faces each day, and she really enjoyed helping people. She'd talk on and on while working on their teeth and then line up the sterilized instruments, ready for the next day. By five o'clock, she knew exactly what she'd accomplished.

But what had she accomplished today? She'd taken care of the baby—bathed, dressed, and fed and fed and fed her. She'd straightened the family room, washed and folded two loads of laundry. Didn't seem like much. But somehow it had consumed her entire day. She hadn't even taken a shower because Marcy woke up just as she turned on the water, and she wasn't yet comfortable taking a shower when the baby was awake.

Only one more month of maternity leave left. How will I ever be able to go back to work when I can't even leave her long enough to take a shower?

This whole subject of going back to work struck a raw spot in Joanie's heart. Should she go back . . . or stay home with Marcy? She didn't know the right answer. John had said they might to able to make it without her salary. But . . . could they? Could she?

Just last night at a reception for John's staff, one man had asked Joanie, "So, what do you do?" She'd thought the answer was perfectly obvious as she'd stood there holding her new baby, but the fact that he had asked made her suspect that "I'm a mom" wouldn't do. So she said, "I'm a dental hygienist." The man had brightened and launched into a few dentist jokes.

What would he have said if I'd told him I'm a mom? Joanie mused.

In her heart, Joanie wanted nothing more than to be home with Marcy and with any other children she and John might have. But in her head . . . she wondered if that would be the right choice. No paycheck. No promotions. No accolades. No to-do list, neatly checked off at the end of each day.

Joanie looked down at Marcy, now sleeping in the crook of her arm and again stroked her soft cheek. Could she do it? This mothering thing? Did mothering really matter enough to invest her life in it?

DOES MOTHERING MATTER?

It's a good question, isn't it? When we're struggling just to get a shower during the daylight hours, we wonder if what we're doing as mothers makes any difference at all. Like darts, negative feelings pierce our confidence and accuse us of insignificance. Take these for example:

I feel that what I do as a mother isn't very important.

It's tough to see much value in wiping applesauce faces, runny noses, and messy bottoms—not just once but over and over again. But every mother was once not a mother. And in her pre-mothering days, she found fulfillment in some aspect of her being. A talent. A career. A sport. A peer group.

Once children come on the scene, however, moms must choose between activities. Many of us opt to care for our babies out of a deep love and desire to meet their needs. But if we're honest, most of us will question—at times—whether or not our choice to "stay home with the kids" is worth it. Moms don't receive report cards or yearly job evaluations. Seldom do we receive a pat on the back or an encouraging word about how we're doing or the difference we're making. In fact,

I used to be able to handle an important career, run a home, and be a reasonably good wife, so I naturally assumed I would be just as effective in mothering. I simply wasn't prepared for this downward spiral of my own self-worth.

— ❧ —

After working outside the home for years and supporting myself, staying home with my new baby made me feel like I wasn't "doing" anything even though I had never worked that hard in my life.

sometimes the kids themselves have a way of puncturing our balloons. "Mom, you're mean," they'll tell us as we attempt to discipline and guide them. Sometimes we wonder.

I feel like I never finish anything!

Erma Bombeck likens the experience of motherhood to that of stringing beads. We go about our daily routine, stringing one brightly colored wooden knob after another, feeling pretty proud of ourselves. We assume we're accomplishing so much. But the illusion of productivity is shattered when, at the end of the day, we look down at our necklace only to discover that there is no knot. The once-strung beads are now scattered all over the place, and we have to start all over.

Comedian Phyllis Diller quips, "Cleaning your house while your kids are still growing is like shoveling the walk before it stops snowing."[1] Other moms agree.

> *I have this frustration that I never finish anything. Picking up toys and doing laundry and making peanut butter and jelly sandwiches and wiping off the kitchen counter . . . it's always there and I'm never done.*
>
> — ❧ —
>
> *Days run into weeks, and life begins to blur into one long monotonous series of chores. . . . With preschoolers, it's difficult to do anything that lasts.*
>
> — ❧ —
>
> *I can't even get the house clean. I get one room done and move on to the next, only to have the first room a disaster again.*

When do moms get to finish anything? We can't finish a meal without getting up and running to the stove, or the refrigerator, or to answer the phone. We scarcely finish a thought before somebody needs something and we've lost our concentration. What's more, finishing a sentence is a rare occurrence.

The very job of mothering is unending. We know that we won't "complete" the assignment of raising our children until they're eighteen, and between infancy and eighteen years is a looooooonnnnngggggg time. Even then, we continue to be Mom, for life.

I feel so exhausted all the time!

Most babies don't sleep through the night in the first several months of life, and many others don't catch on for the entire first year or even longer! Once they finally settle into some kind of decent pattern, other challenges kick in. Like disciplining a two-year-old, potty-

> *After spending nine long, hard months waiting for my son's birth, I thought his arrival would be a relief. In some ways it was, but I was utterly unprepared for the difficulty of getting little sleep and still having so much to do. I never expected that caring for a newborn would be so all-encompassing. And no matter how much I love my son, I still have a hard time functioning on so little sleep.*

training, and answering questions, questions, questions. It's been said that life with a newborn is exhausting physically. And life with a toddler is exhausting mentally and emotionally.

I feel so out of control!

Suddenly those who used to enjoy a sense of order in their days experience bedlam. How do you control your schedule when a baby comes down with an ear infection, or when he messes through his diaper just as you're ready to walk out the door for church, or when she trips and falls and everything comes to a screeching halt while you bandage a boo-boo? How do you stay in charge of a home that formerly belonged to you but has now been invaded by others who have stuff that never seems to stay in place? How do you go from the freedom of doing *what* you want *when* you want . . . to a total lack of freedom?

Does mothering matter? It's a question that demands an answer. We live in a day when what you do equals who you are. A woman's worth is determined by the value of her work and the amount she accomplishes. And if your work is constantly unfinished or coming undone, is exhausting or without tangible reward, you question your worth.

I'm a very organized person. I like everything in place. Before we had children, that's how things were. Now I look around and see all those toys—a huge mess—not made by me.

I don't feel important. Sometimes, when I spend the day running errands, cleaning, carpooling, and making meals, I begin to think that anyone could do what I'm doing. . . . I'm not so important.

— ❧ —

In tears one night, I began to wonder what I do that is worthwhile. I don't work or go to school. I do chores—clean the house, do laundry, cook—and all of these are undone by the end of the day. I organize an event and no one even notices. How is my life going to count?

Anne Morrow Lindbergh in her classic, *Gift From the Sea,* describes a woman's dilemma in this way:

> In the job of home-keeping there is no raise from the boss, and seldom praise from others to show us we have hit the

mark. Except for the child, woman's creation is so often invisible, especially today. We are working at an arrangement in form, of the myriad disparate details of housework, family routine, and social life. It is a kind of intricate game of cat's cradle we manipulate on our fingers, with invisible threads. How can one point to this constant tangle of household chores, errands, and fragments of human relationships, as a creation? It is hard even to think of it as purposeful activity, so much of it is automatic. Woman herself begins to feel like a telephone exchange or a laundromat.[2]

One mother of young children, tired of feeling insignificant, decided to prove to her husband that what she did *mattered* by simply not doing it for one whole day. "What happened here today?" he asked when he walked into a kitchen strewn with dirty dishes, half-eaten sandwiches, and spilled cereal. Sitting on a couch amid the clutter of toys and newspapers, she replied, "You're always asking me what I do all day, so I decided not to do it."

WHAT "THEY" SAY ABOUT MOTHERING

Perhaps the need for significance is so great in the mother of young children because she is surrounded on all sides by a culture that is itself confused about the value of mothering. In the past fifty years, opinions about a woman's worth and the value of motherhood have changed greatly.

In the '40s, women moved into the workforce to help out during World War II. In the '50s, they returned home to make the family the center of their attention. In the '60s, the Women's Movement blossomed, and in the '70s and '80s, women combined home and office in discovering equal worth with men. In the late '80s and early '90s, women realized they'd left something out in their pursuit of identity and began to explore the meaning of femininity in all its roles. Today, women work to make their families fit in with who they are, and who they are fit in with their families.

While the pendulum swings, mothers puzzle over the worth of their work. Some toil at mothering from dawn until dusk, with home as their sole place of vocation. Others delegate some maternal responsibilities to others for parts of the day or night. But all who mother face the challenge of investing time and energy in the lives of their children.

From wherever we live with our infants, our toddlers, our grade-schoolers and our teenagers, the world around us walls us in with two clear messages.

Mothering is not viewed as a "job."

If you mother, and only mother, society says you don't work. And even if you mother while lawyering, wallpapering, or running a bookkeeping service from your home office, the mothering part of your day isn't valued as "work."

A while back, the state of California officially informed one mother who wanted to run for Congress that motherhood didn't count as a job. Because mothers don't receive pay for their work, mothering was not recognized as an occupation on the ballot.

Nope. Mothering isn't a job. It's a biological status. Like womanhood. Like childhood. You mother. Around the clock. In the wee hours of the night and then again at the crack of dawn. When you're sick and when you're healthy. Whether you feel like it or whether you don't. You mother. But you don't work at mothering.

You won't find mothering listed on the employment resumés of most women, even though most women are mothers and have mothered for many years. And while it may be the work most faithfully completed, day in and day out, during the sum of a woman's life, you won't often see it listed in an obituary.

Mothering isn't viewed by our society as work. For that matter, neither is fathering. The task of raising and tending a family is not valued by our world. So it's pretty tough to value our major investment in life when the culture in which we live judges it as "unwork." By logical conclusion, what is unwork is leisure. Or optional. Or easy. In any case, it doesn't matter much. It's not significant and doesn't provide a person with a sense of worth.

Mothering is not valued as a skill.

In our culture today, being a mother is like living at the low end of the food chain. As Joan France remarks in *Newsweek*, "This society neither respects nor rewards nurturing skills."[3] Take a look at the job vacancies in the United States today. Big gaps are growing in all service professions, with nursing and teaching experiencing gaping holes.

Mothering skills, where time and energy are invested in the lives of those who cannot do for themselves, are undervalued as well. One newspaper reported a woman, teeter-tottering in her decision to start a family, saying, "My husband and I are trying to decide whether to get a dog or have a child. We haven't decided whether to ruin our carpets or to ruin our lives."

Sylvia Ann Hewlett, author of *When the Bough Breaks*, suggests that current legislation proves that nurturing skills are not valued. She asserts that most states give more attention to regulating dog kennels than day care centers.

All around us are the blatant messages that mothering is no more than an expensive hobby. Little praise or encouragement is given to those who invest their lives in the lives of children, trading personal fulfillment for the well-being of future adults.

Brenda Hunter, author of *Where Have All the Mothers Gone?* and *The Company of Women*, declares that "our culture tells mothers they are not that important in their children's lives. For three decades, mothering has been devalued in America. It has even become a status symbol for the modern woman to take as little time as possible away from work for full-time mothering."[4]

The message is strong. Mothering isn't

I need to know that what I'm doing has purpose and is important. I'll wait years before I see any results.

— ❧ —

I need affirmation that the choices I have made are worth it, especially when I cleaned the kitchen floor for the third time that day or stayed home with a sick child.

viewed as a job nor valued as a skill. No wonder mothers wonder if mothering matters. No wonder many mothers question their significance.

THE DIFFERENCE THAT MOTHERING MAKES

In order to truly see the difference that mothering makes, we must learn to redefine the worth of mothering. It is not defined by a paycheck or a promotion. The value of mothering is discovered in the peace of mind that comes when you know you are doing all you can do with all you've been given. Mothering makes a difference in several areas.

Mothering makes a difference in the life of your child.

You are the mother your child needs. God has chosen you for the job. No one else in the world can mean as much to your child as you.

You make a difference in the physical development of your child.

Early childhood is a critical time. In fact, according to new scientific evidence, these fleeting years are even more crucial than we once realized. Reports now tell us that a child's environment from birth to age three helps determine brain structure and ability to learn.

A 1994 Carnegie Corporation report finds that brain development before age one is:

- more rapid and extensive,
- more vulnerable to environmental influence, and
- longer-lasting than previously realized.

The study further states that:

- The environment affects the number of brain cells, connections among them, and the way connections are wired.
- Early stress has a negative impact on brain development.

This three-year study concludes that millions of infants and toddlers are so deprived of medical care, loving support, and intellectual stimulation that their growth into healthy adulthood is threatened.[5] Your mothering matters to the physical development of your child.

You make a difference in the emotional development of your child.

Your child's ability to learn as well as her ability to love is influenced at this early age. A mother's nurturing love builds the foundation of the child's ability to love others, to learn, and to adjust to his or her environment.

Speaking at the 1994 MOPS International Leadership Convention, child expert and author Jeanne Hendricks said, "To the newborn child, people are everything. The earliest social skill is when that little infant can find and hold the eyes of an adult in what we call the 'quiet-alert' stage. And you never forget it once you've experienced it. It's when that little one looks at you and says, 'Can I trust you?' Because the first developmental task of a newborn child is to find out, 'Is this a safe world? Am I going to be accepted and loved?'"

Along similar lines, other child-development experts tell us that it is secure attachment with the mother that forms the foundation for the child's entire self-structure and identity. A parent and child work together to create an individual who can look in a mirror and squeal with delight, "That's me!" According to Assistant Professor of Psychology at the University of Colorado, Sandra Pipp, "Infants who are securely attached to their mothers and fathers have a more complex knowledge of themselves and others than insecurely attached infants. Children from one to three years of age who are more securely attached are able to relate to themselves and their parents in more ways than those who are insecurely attached."[6]

Writing one hundred years ago, Sigmund Freud described the relationship of a young child to his mother as "unique, without parallel, established unalterably for a whole lifetime as the first and strongest love object and as the prototype of all later love relationships for both sexes."[7] Even earlier, these words appeared in Plato's *Republic:* "You know that the beginning is the most important part of any work, especially in the care of a young and tender thing; for that is the time at which the character is being formed and the desired impression is more readily taken."

The mother not only feeds the physical being but also the emotional self and soul of the child. When we downplay the contribution of the mother in the life of a child, especially in the early years, we simply ignore her vital role in that child's development. Dr. Marianne Neifert, known to millions as "Dr. Mom," looks back at her own inadequate presence for bonding in the lives of some of her children and boldly asserts, "There is something terribly abnormal about separating mothers from their babies. We must stop glamorizing it. . . . A baby has some rights to her mother."[8]

Mothering makes a difference in the life of the mother.

In the adjustment to becoming a mother, we often don't understand the difference our efforts make. But bit by bit, the impact of our lives on those of our children becomes clearer.

Does it matter if a mother rolls over and goes back to sleep, ignoring her three-month-old who wakens at two o'clock in the morning? Does it matter if a mother sits on the front porch and watches her toddler follow a ball into the busy street, without running to stop him at the curb? Does it matter if a mother ignores another straight A report card from her perfectionistic eleven-year-old daughter because, after all, she always makes straight A's? Does it matter if a mother obeys the closed door rule of silence imposed on her by a teenage son in whose drawer she has found what looks like cocaine?

Mothering matters. And if we invest ourselves in the formative years when a child is dependent upon parents for his or her development, we will reap the benefits later in life with the joy of living with a more secure and independent child.

In her address to the 1990 graduating class of Wellesley College, this line drew then-First Lady Barbara Bush the most fervent applause: "At the end of your life, you'll never regret not having passed one more test, not winning one more verdict, or not closing one more deal. You will regret times not spent with a husband, a friend, a child, or a parent."

Mothering makes a difference in the world.

At MOPS International, we're fond of the motto that mothering matters . . . because "today makes a difference tomorrow." We've become accustomed to applying that sentiment to the maintenance of our planet. Most of us have become knowledgeable and skilled at recycling plastic milk bottles, and glass jelly jars. Empty aluminum cans sit in bags in garages to be exchanged for pennies at the grocery store. There are even those among us who reuse shopping bags and have converted our toilets with water-saving devices.

We would be wise to transfer this truth—that today makes a difference tomorrow—to our mothering. As Jeanne Hendricks concluded her speech to MOPS leaders in 1994, she warned that we are more concerned about making a better world for our children than we are about making better children for our world. Mothering matters not only to the child and to the mother, but also to the world in which they live. In fact, Leo Tolstoy in *The Lion and the Honeycomb* writes, "Yes, women, mothers, in your hands more than in those of anyone else lies the salvation of the world." ?

BUILDING BLOCKS

BUILDING BLOCK #1:

Create your own job description as a mother.

Write out a job description for yourself as a mother. One mom describes the necessary qualifications this way: "Full-time motherhood requires the creativity of Thomas Edison, the diplomacy of Henry Kissinger, and the patience of Mother Teresa."[9]

A MOPS group in Hamilton, New Zealand, wrote the following description, worded like a classified ad:

SITUATIONS VACANT: HOUSEWIFE/ MOTHER

Applications are invited for the position of manager to a lively team of four demanding individuals.

The successful applicant will be required to perform the following functions: companion, counselor, financial manager, buying officer, teacher, nurse, chef, nutritionist, decorator, cleaner, driver, child care supervisor, social secretary, and recreation officer. Applicants must have unlimited energy and a strong sense of responsibility. They must be independent, self-motivated and able to work in isolation without supervision, able to work under stress, and adaptable enough to handle new developments in the life of the team, including emergencies and crises. They must be able to communicate with people of all ages, including teachers, doctors, business people, dentists, teenagers and children. A good imagination, sensitivity, warmth, and an understanding of people is necessary as the successful applicant will also be responsible for the mental and emotional well-being of the team.

HOURS: All waking moments and a 24-hour shift when necessary.

BENEFITS: No guaranteed holidays, no sick leave or maternity leave. No workers' compensation.

PAY: None. Allowances by arrangement from time to time with the income-earning member of the team. Successful applicant may be allowed/required to hold second job in addition to the one advertised here.

How would you change or rewrite this ad? Does it help you realize your value and abilities?

BUILDING BLOCK #2:

List the skills acquired through mothering.

We sometimes imagine we're doing "nothing of significance" when so much of our time is spent in unmeasurable activities. Yet, when you take the time to catalog all that you are gaining, you'll be encouraged by how mothering is, indeed, building skills. Determine which of the following qualities you possess already and then add others to the list:

- The ability to work without supervision, often under stress and with frequent distractions.
- The ability to communicate well with people of all ages and education levels.
- The ability to be resourceful and to plan and coordinate the activities of several different people.
- The ability to handle conflict with patience.[10]

BUILDING BLOCK #3:

Learn to view yourself as a "key person."

The next time you're tempted to think you aren't worth very much or that what you're doing as a mother isn't important, consider the following:

You Are a Key Person

Xvxn though my typxwritxr is an old modxl, it works vxry wxll xxcxpt for onx kxy. You would think that with all thx othxr kxys functioning properly, onx kxy not working would hardly bx noticxd, but just onx kxy out of whack sxxms to ruin thx wholx xffort.

You may say to yoursxlf, "Wxll, I'm only onx pxrson, no onx will xvxn noticx if I don't quitx do my bxst."

But it doxs makx a diffxrxnc bxcausx to bx xffxctivx an organization nxxds activx participation by xvxryonx to the bxst of his and hxr ability.

So thx nxxt timx you think you arx not important rxmxmbxr my old typxwritxr.

You arx a kxy pxrson![11]

The next time you feel insignificant, "x" yourself out of the picture. What's wrong with that picture? "X" yourself out of Christmas preparations or just-wake-up-in-the-morning times, and what is missing? You are a key person. You are the mother of your children because God has chosen you for them.

BUILDING BLOCK #4:

God values mothers.

Of the infinite number of creative possibilities, God created the model of families, where children are born and nurtured and where mothers play a key role. Check the models of mothers in the Bible: Eve (Gen. 1); Sarah (Gen. 16–18); Hannah (1 Sam. 1), and Mary (Luke 1).

- Do you think these women ever questioned their value as mothers?
- How does God show he values these and all mothers through these models?

BUILDING BLOCK #5:

Children value mothers.

In a moment when you wonder whether you matter to your children, read this:

> Everybody knows that a good mother gives her children a feeling of trust and stability. She is the one they can count on for the things that matter most of all. She is their food and their bed and their extra blanket when it grows cold in the night; she is their warmth and health and their shelter; she is the one they want to be near when they cry. She is the only person in the whole world, or in a whole lifetime, who can be these things to her children. There is no substitute for her. Somehow even her clothes feel different to her children's hands from anybody else's clothes. Only to touch her skirt or her sleeve makes a troubled child feel better.

> *—The Journal and Letters of the Little Locksmith*
> Katherine Butler Hathaway

FOR FURTHER READING:

Getting Out of Your Kids' Faces and Into Their Hearts, Valerie Bell

Home by Choice, Brenda Hunter, Ph.D.

A Mother's Legacy, Jeanne Hendricks

Mom, You're Incredible! Linda Weber

A Season at Home, Debbie Barr

Sometimes I Feel Like Running Away from Home, Elizabeth Cody Newenhuyse

Mom to Mom, Elisa Morgan (February 1996 release)

Where Have All the Mothers Gone? Brenda Hunter, Ph.D.

Mothering Maxim

— ❦ —

Mothering matters ...
because today makes a
difference tomorrow.

Identity:

Sometimes I'm not sure who I am

S he shifted the weight of the infant seat to one hip and used it to prop open the door to the hair salon as her three-year-old passed through. "Whew!" Cheryl exclaimed as she set down her load and began taking coats off both the toddler and the baby. "I made it!" she told the receptionist with a laugh. "I wasn't so sure about an hour ago. I got everybody dressed, and then Bryan spilled Cheerios® and milk all over the kitchen floor and himself, and four-month-old Allison blew out her diaper. So we had to start all over again. But here we are—and only five minutes late. Not bad!"

The receptionist smiled and led Cheryl, Bryan, and baby Allison back to Patti, who greeted the gang with gusto. "Hey, Bryan! Here's a special spot for you. You can entertain your little sister while I cut your mom's hair. Okay, buddy?"

Bryan beamed with the recognition of his role as Big Brother and settled in above his still-strapped-in sister and began talking to her in cooing tones.

"I'm so glad to be here," Cheryl told Patti. "My hair has been driving me nuts. I only hope the kids will hold up for the next fifteen minutes."

"They'll be fine," Patti assured her. "You've got such great kids," she added as she laid Cheryl back in the chair to wash her hair.

As Patti lathered her head, the compliment oozed into Cheryl's tired muscles like a soothing ointment. They *were* good kids, and she loved them more than life itself.

Rinsed and toweled, Cheryl stepped over some toys to the styling chair, where Patti clipped on an apron and then was called to the telephone. "I'll be back in a sec," she said, spinning Cheryl around to face the mirror.

In the reflection, Cheryl could see Bryan playing with Allison. He bent over her and clicked his tongue at his baby sister, just like Cheryl did. The infant giggled and wriggled in her seat. Cheryl smiled and shifted her gaze to her own face in the mirror.

Ugh! she thought. *I should have put on some makeup. But there wasn't time. There never is, anymore.* She sighed, staring at her face. When was the last time she'd really *looked* at herself? With her wet hair slicked back from her face, she could see new creases in her forehead. She hardly recognized herself. *Is this what I look like now?* she wondered.

Then suddenly, surprisingly, she felt a weird chill as she saw staring back at her not just a tired mom or an older version of herself—but someone else, someone who looked familiar and yet couldn't be identified. She peered closer. It wasn't so much any particular feature, but the expression, the whole package. And then she knew. Staring back at her from the reflection in the mirror was the face of her mother.

She drew in her breath quickly, checked on Bryan and Allison, and then took another look in the mirror. *Who are you?* she wondered to the face in the mirror. *Who am I anymore?*

I'M NOT SURE WHO I AM

Whether we're twelve or twenty, thirty-two or forty-seven, we keep asking ourselves, "Who am I?" In some stages of life, we embrace the question willingly and engage in a mental wrestling match until we reach a satisfying answer. But for the mother of young children, the question can seem a bit

Who am I? Ha! That's easy, right? I'm a mom. I'm a wife. I'm a need-meeter. I'm a cook. I'm a milk-machine. I'm a laundromat. I'm tired. I'm ... not sure anymore.

threatening. All tangled up with our roles and responsibilities, the answer is elusive.

> *I didn't know I'd have to give up so much of myself.*
>
> — ❧ —
>
> *I'm about ninety-nine percent mom and only one percent myself.*

As new mothers, we need to redefine ourselves. We need to find and accept the kind of definition that will sustain us during this season when we are pulled and stretched and drained and sometimes overwhelmed by the responsibility of taking care of others. Though most of us enjoy what we're doing, we're like Cheryl who was suddenly confronted with the question that all new mothers inevitably ask, "Who am I *now?*"

WHO AM I?

A mother tends to define herself most easily in terms of her external circumstances. She looks in the mirror and, instead of seeing her reflection as an identity in its own right, she sees the various facets of her life staring back at her.

> *I sometimes fear I will wake up one day and totally forget who I am; that I will lose all my identity to all those roles I fulfill twenty-four hours a day, seven days a week.*
>
> — ❧ —
>
> *This mom thing has really shaken me to the core. I don't have a clue who I am—even after five personality tests. There's a looming feeling that if I don't figure it out soon, I'm going to ruin three young lives.*

I am what I do.

When she goes to a school event or sits next to a stranger in church who asks, "What do you do?" a woman is likely to label herself in terms of a relationship or a job description—"I'm Beth's mom"; "I'm Tom's wife"; "I'm an accountant"; "I'm a part-time consultant."

For moms who stay home with their children, this common ice-breaker often causes them to cringe:

> *I make a new friend who hands me her business card and then asks me what I do, and I don't know what to say.*

One stay-at-home mom attended a fancy dinner party with her husband. As they mingled with many of his clients, she heard people defining themselves with important job titles. So she armed herself with a powerful answer. Sure enough, someone finally asked her: "And what do *you* do?"

"I'm the CEO of my family!" she shot back proudly.

I am what others need me to be.

This season of life is a season of self-sacrifice, but as moms, we often lose our identities in the overwhelming desire or sense of responsibility to be a need-meeter.

It's as if we cease to exist for anything other than meeting the needs of others, and we not only begin to identify ourselves in that way, but we begin to measure our value and worth by our ability to meet those needs. If my baby is good (sleeps through the night, learns to crawl or walk on schedule, interacts well with other children), then I tell myself that I have met his needs and I am good. If my baby is bad (screams when I leave the room, hits other children, or flushes my watch down the toilet), then I accuse myself of not meeting her needs and I am bad.

My baby began to control my life, even before she was born, directing me from the womb with demands like, "Eat now! Rest more! Drink more water! Don't eat that!"

— ❧ —

I'm surprised that I'm so consumed by my children and their needs.

— ❧ —

My baby takes up all of my day — and all of my self.

For the mother who is also a wife, meeting the needs of her husband can also preempt her own identity. She is the one who listens to his dreams. She is the source of his inspirations and passion. She is the caretaker who makes sure he has clean shirts and socks. She advises him in his interactions with the children as well as those he has with their couple-friends. Therefore, when he succeeds, she succeeds. When he fails, she fails. What he thinks becomes what she thinks. Her identity can become an extension of his.

While this may sound like an oversimplification, we often do get our identities confused with the role of need-meeter.

I am what I accomplish.

As stated in the last chapter on significance, many of us believe that who we are equals what we accomplish. "I'm a painter; here are my pictures." Or, "I'm an accountant; here is my Rolodex of clients." We are validated by the results of our efforts. In a stage of life where we may accomplish little more than getting to the grocery store or keeping up with the dirty dishes and diapers, an identity based on accomplishment is an identity at risk.

I am what I've experienced.

Another partial picture of identity is taken from the past. From the time we feed as infants in our mother's arms and focus on her eyes, only inches from our own, we are drinking in messages about who we are. She becomes the mirror that gives us our identity. In her praise and criticism, patience and impatience, approval and disapproval, we develop an image of who we are. So, too, with our father. He comes home, drops his briefcase and lifts us in the air, mirroring back to us how important we are to him. Or he brushes us aside to concentrate on the newspaper, and we conclude that we are of no value at all.

Siblings and our birth order among them in the family describe our place in the scheme of life. As firstborns, we often see a reflection of superiority in our first-place rankings. As second-borns, we see competition and conditional love in the eyes of the one above us. Opposite-sex siblings challenge our sexual identity while same-sex siblings underline it.

And those of us who experienced some trauma in our past often live with wounded identities in the present. Like a whirling mirror-ball suspended from the ceiling of a dance floor, the painful past scatters the shards of broken images, leaving us unsure of who we were, who we are, and who we will become.

All of these mirrors offer only pieces of our identity. Even the combination of our responsibilities, our activities, and our past is not enough. Who we are is larger than any one of these and more than their combination.

WHO AM I *NOT*?

While the mirrors around us reflect an incomplete picture of identity, they can also offer inaccurate reflections, confusing our understanding of who we are. Gregg Lewis observes, "Often the picture we get of ourselves from the outside world is as distorted as the bizarre reflection you might see in a House of Mirrors at a county fair."[1]

To understand who we are, we have to come to grips with who we are *not*.

I am not my children.

In this season of constant giving, when our children are nearly totally dependent upon us, we derive some sense of value from their responses and accomplishments, but the lines separating us can grow fuzzy. We have to remind ourselves that we are separate. The goal of our role as mothers, in fact, is to continually strengthen that separateness. As psychologist Erik Fromm writes, "In motherly love, two people who were one become separate."[2]

Though I love my children and am proud of them, their accomplishments are not my report card, nor their shortfalls my failure. I can't wrap my ego around them.

— 🐚 —

I feel strange now when I go out without the kids (which is rare) ... like I'm not as important alone.

— 🐚 —

In this all-consuming new role of mothering, I fear that I've lost me. I live through my children. My self-esteem is going!

I am not my mother.

Perhaps one of the greatest shocks of mothering is looking at ourselves and seeing the traits of our own mothers: "In giving birth, a woman suddenly confronts her parenting history. She reflects on her early childhood as she cares for her baby. Moreover, a woman identifies with her own mother when she becomes a mother for the first time."[3]

Mothers of young children must process this stage of identity development. Yes, each of us possesses some of the qualities of our own mothers. But, at the same time, each of us is unique. A pivotal truth is that "similar to" does not mean "the same as." While you may have inherited your mother's bone structure, you do not necessarily have her temper. While you may have picked up a creative streak from her, you don't have to repeat her habit of negative nagging.

You may be like your mother in some ways, but you are *not* your mother. Nor are you your mother-in-law, your grandmother, or your stepmother.

I am not my sister, my neighbor, or any other woman.

Sure, your older sister has this mothering thing down pat. She's been at it for eight years longer than you have. And your super-mom neighbor probably just *looks* like she knows what she's doing. But I'll bet that beneath her well-applied makeup and well-maintained house, she still struggles with some aspect of her day. Don't let her fool you.

To "compare" means to examine characteristics and qualities in order to determine differences and similarities. That's healthy; we can all improve on certain qualities and skills. But when we use comparisons to determine our personal worth, we're looking in the wrong direction. Your value is not dependent upon how you stack up next to someone else. You are not your sister, your neighbor, or anyone else you admire.

SO WHO AM I REALLY?

If you're more than the sum of your responsibilities and relationships, your accomplishments and your past, and you know who you are not, then who are you, really? The question still begs an answer, and the truth is simpler, greater, and more enduring than all these partial or inaccurate reflections.

Our true identity comes not from looking into horizontal mirrors—at reflections of ourselves or our mothers or our past—but looking up at God. As we gaze into his face, we begin to get a true picture of ourselves. He created us in his image.

In his book, *Life Mapping,* John Trent puts it this way:

> Did you know that there's a miraculous mirror you can go to anytime that will reflect the brightest and best part of you? It's a mirror not of make-believe ... but one of rock-solid reality. Just open your Bible to 2 Corinthians 3:18 and you'll find a mirror that can reveal your strengths and point you toward the person you'd most like to become.[4]

In his book, *The Sensation of Being Somebody,* Maurice Wagner suggests that all images bear some relationship to the object they represent. In other words, God created us to represent him; he put his thumbprint upon our beings, and through our relationship with him, we begin to know and understand and accept ourselves. For some, this is a challenging process.

I'm not who I thought I was. I've been operating from behind masks of who I wanted to be most of my teenage and adult years. But now God is holding a mirror before me, helping me to see who I really am.

The goal is to know our true identity in God's eyes because the Bible promises that the truth will set us free (John 8:32). The Bible gives us three foundational truths that tell us who we are. As you read them, consider how they apply to you.

I am unique.

God creates each of us as a unique being. You are *you*—a unique combination of personality traits, physical makeup, talents, and abilities. You are either an extrovert or an introvert, a morning or night person, type A or B on the stress scale, small- or large-boned; the list could go on. Others may have similar traits, but no one is packaged exactly like you. God has created you uniquely ... to be who you are.

Need scientific proof? Law enforcement experts have long used the technique of identifying people by means of their fingerprints, because no two are the same. Today, research in DNA reveals that the smallest of body parts (hair samples or skin flakes, for example) can identify individuals with equal accuracy.

Mothers are quick to recognize the uniqueness of their children. No two siblings are exactly alike. Though both are brought up in the same environment, one may be strong-willed while the other is compliant. One loves all foods; the other is picky. Yet are you as quick to acknowledge and accept your own uniqueness? Each of you represents a unique combination of heredity and environment that, woven together, forms the framework of who you are, created in God's image, for his unique purpose.

You are unique.

I am imperfect.

Each of us, no matter how hard we try, falls short of perfection, and this imperfection is most often revealed within the context of our close relationships. We try to be good mothers, but sometimes what we see surprises—and disappoints—us.

What we discover in our most intimate relationships is that we are not perfect, but the comforting truth is that God knows about our imperfections. In fact, that's the reason he sent his Son, Jesus, to die on the cross—to forgive us for our "imperfectness." Living in the reality of that forgiveness gives us the strength to keep going, to forgive ourselves, and to accept ourselves.

I'm not who I thought I was. I wanted to be a perfect mom.

— ❧ —

What surprises me most about being a mother is myself. My temper and impatience with my kids.

"Indeed, the struggle of self-acceptance is, in a strong sense, a case of disillusionment," writes Martha Thatcher. "We may be disappointed in our character, our abilities, or our role in life; we had thought it would all be quite different. No matter how many good points about ourselves we become aware of, we are still disappointed in what is not there."[5]

Coming to grips with who we are doesn't mean that we wallow in our imperfections. We don't have to replay negative messages over and over in our minds, brainwashing ourselves about what we lack in order to know ourselves. But coming to see ourselves in truth requires that we take off any masks of denial and admit our inadequacies. They, too, help us define ourselves.

In his book, *The Art of Learning to Love Yourself,* Cecil Osborne writes, "The people I know who truly like themselves as persons, apart from their roles in life as husband, wife, parent or job-holder, are those who have learned to be honest with themselves and who to some degree understand themselves."[6]

You are imperfect. You are fallible human beings who are in process. You will make mistakes; you will lose your patience; you will sometimes act unlovingly.

I am loved.

God loves us unconditionally—without regard to our performance or goodness or consistent ability to be good mothers.

One of the best-known verses of the Bible is John 3:16: "For God so loved the world that he gave his one and only Son, that whoever believes in him shall not perish but have eternal life."

Substitute your own name for *the world* in this verse, and you'll have a true message of God's love for you. In simplest terms, God assures us that we are loved. Each one of us. In fact, we are so very loved that God Himself died for us on the cross.

So whether or not your mother loved you, your child tells you you're special, or your husband says it often enough, the truth is, you are loved.

GETTING TO KNOW ME

Learning to apply these truths in our lives as mothers of young children is a process. In a simple checklist, here's what these truths mean:

We need to know ourselves the way God knows us.

If we know ourselves—recognizing our uniqueness and our imperfections—and know that God loves us, we are free to accept ourselves. We are even free to love ourselves. God tells us to love our neighbors *as ourselves* (Matt. 22:39). This is not a prideful type of self-love. Rather, it is a secure acceptance of ourselves. It is seeing ourselves as God sees us. This is our true identity, which sets us free from guilt and self-consciousness and put-downs. This self-acceptance meets a critical need that moms have.

We need to care for ourselves for the sake of our children.

Author and mother Valerie Bell exhorts, "Becoming a parent should motivate moms and dads to care for themselves emotionally. Sometimes we meet our children's needs by meeting our own needs. It seems like a paradox, but it's true. *Take care of your emotional health for the sake of your child.* If you love your child, you should be willing to do any preventive work that keeps you from passing on your own problems to your child. And along the way, you will be doing yourself an enormous favor as well."[7]

We need to accept ourselves for the sake of our children.

Valerie Bell goes on to say, "It's hard for a child to trust an adult who is like an emotional yo-yo—loving one minute, angry and explosive the next. An unpredictable parent, one given to wide emotional swings, is an unstable parent."[8]

We need to accept ourselves for the sake of others around us.

As stated, the Golden Rule tells us to love our neighbor as ourselves. The very core of the rule requires that we love ourselves. For if, in fact, we do not love ourselves, we are unable to truly love others.

Who am I? The question keeps popping up as we grow and change. Which mirror gives the truest answer, the one that will sustain us through changing circumstances and changing roles?

Horizontal mirrors will help you to know parts of yourself as you look to your families and your past for answers. But it is the vertical mirror—gazing at God—that gives you the truest reflections of yourself. God reminds you who you are. He tells you the truth that sets you free to know yourself, to accept yourself, and therefore to be yourself. ❧

BUILDING BLOCKS

BUILDING BLOCK #1:

Get to know yourself.

In his book, *That Incredible Christian,* A. W. Tozer writes about the importance of self-discovery:

That God already knows us thoroughly is certain (Ps. 139:1–6). It remains for us to know ourselves as accurately as possible. For this reason I offer some rules for self-discovery; and if the results are not all we could desire, they may be at least better than none at all. We may be known by the following:

- *What we want most.* We have but to get quiet, recollect our thoughts, wait for the mild excitement within us to subside, and then listen closely for the faint cry of desire. Ask your heart: What would you rather have than anything else in the world? Reject the conventional answer. Insist on the true one, and when you have heard it, you will know the kind of person you are.

- *What we think about most.* The necessities of life compel us to think about many things, but the true test is what we think about voluntarily. It is more than likely that our thoughts will cluster about our secret heart treasure, and whatever that is will reveal what we are. "Where your treasure is, there will your heart be also."

- *How we use our money.* Again we must ignore those matters about which we are not altogether free. We must pay taxes and provide the necessities of life for ourselves and family, if any. That is routine, merely, and tells us little about ourselves. But whatever money is left to do with as we please—that will tell us a great deal indeed.

- *What we do with our leisure time.* A large share of our time is already spoken for by the exigencies of civilized living, but we do have some free time. What we do with it is vital. Most people waste it staring at the television, listening to the radio, reading the cheap output of the press, or engaging in idle chatter. What I do with mine reveals the kind of person I am.

- *The company we enjoy.* There is a law of moral attraction that draws every person to the society most like their self. "Being let go, they went to their own company." Where we go when we are free to go where we will is a near infallible index of character.

- *Whom we admire.* I have long suspected that the great majority of evangelical Christians, while kept somewhat in line by the pressure of group opinion, nevertheless have a boundless, if perforce, secret admiration for the world. We can learn the true state of our minds by examining our unexpressed admirations. Israel often admired, even envied, the pagan nations around them, and so forgot the law and the promises and the fathers. Instead of blaming Israel, let us look to ourselves.[9]

Self-Examination: Ask yourself some tough questions:

- How well do you know yourself? What are your greatest strengths? Greatest weaknesses? What three adjectives best describe you?
- If you were to see yourself as God sees you, how would your opinion of yourself be different?
- When asked what moms need most, many said "acceptance." Do you accept yourself? Do you believe that God does? Do you think you're the one exception to God's great love?

BUILDING BLOCK #2:

Take a personality test.

Following are four lists of adjectives. Circle the ones that describe you and tally your score below each box.

Box 1	
Takes charge	Enterprising
Self-reliant	Determined
Assertive	Firm
Competitive	Bold
Enjoys challenges	Purposeful
Decision-maker	Leader
Goal-driven	Adventurous
"Let's do it now!"	

Box 2	
Takes risks	Fun-loving
Visionary	Creative
Motivator	Energetic
Very verbal	Promoter
Avoids details	Likes variety
Enjoys change	Mixes easily
Group-oriented	Optimistic
"Trust me. It'll work out."	

Box 3	
Loyal	Nurturing
Nondemanding	Even keel
Good listener	Tolerant
Avoids conflict	Thoughtful
Enjoys routine	Adaptable
Dislikes change	Sympathetic
Deep relationships	Patient
"Let's keep things the way they are."	

Box 4	
Deliberate	Orderly
Controlled	Discerning
Reserved	Analytical
Predictable	Precise
Practical	Factual
Detailed	Inquisitive
Persistent	Scheduled
"How was it done in the past?"	

Which "box" are you, based on your highest score? Author John Trent likens these personality qualities to four different animals in his children's book, *The Treasure Tree*. Here are the descriptions:

Box 1: Lion

1. Is daring and unafraid in new situations.
2. Likes to be a leader. Often tells others how to do things.
3. Ready to take on any kind of challenge.
4. Is firm and serious about what is expected.
5. Makes decisions quickly.

Box 2: Otter

1. Talks a lot and tells wild stories.
2. Likes to do all kinds of fun things.
3. Enjoys being in groups. Likes to perform.
4. Full of energy and always eager to play.
5. Always happy and sees the good part of everything.

Box 3: Golden Retriever

1. Always loyal and faithful to friends.
2. Listens carefully to others.
3. Likes to help others. Feels sad when others are hurt.
4. Is a peacemaker. Doesn't like it when others argue.
5. Patient and willing to wait for something.

Box 4: Beaver

1. Is neat and tidy and notices little details.
2. Sticks with something until it's done. Doesn't like to quit in the middle of a game.
3. Asks lots of questions.
4. Likes things done the same way.
5. Tells things just the way they are.[10]

M BUILDING BLOCK #3:

Get to know God's view of you.

Who does God say I am?

I am made in the image of God (Gen. 1:26–27).

I am a child of God (John 1:12).

I am a temple—a dwelling place—of God. His Spirit and his life dwell in me (1 Cor. 3:16).

I am a saint (Eph. 1:1; 1 Cor. 1:2; Phil. 1:1; Col. 1:2).

I am righteous and holy (Eph. 4:24).

I am chosen and appointed by Christ to bear his fruit (John 15:16).

I am God's workmanship—his handiwork—born anew in Christ to do his work (Eph. 2:10).

I am chosen of God, holy and dearly loved (Col. 3:12; 1 Thess. 1:4).

I am a child of God, and I will resemble Christ when he returns (1 John 3:1–2).

I am fearfully and wonderfully made (Ps. 139:14).

♣ BUILDING BLOCK #4:

Realize that God loves you.

Because God Loves Me (1 Cor. 13:4–8)

Because God loves me, he is slow to lose patience with me.

Because God loves me, he takes the circumstances of my life and uses them in a constructive way for my growth.

Because God loves me, he does not treat me as an object to be possessed and manipulated.

Because God loves me, he has no need to impress me with how great and powerful he is because *he is God*, nor does he belittle me as his child in order to show me how important he is.

Because God loves me, he is for me. He wants to see me mature and develop in his love.

Because God loves me, he does not send down his wrath on every little mistake I make, of which there are many.

Because God loves me, he does not keep score of all my sins and then beat me over the head with them whenever he gets the chance.

Because God loves me, he is deeply grieved when I do not walk in the ways that please him because he sees this as evidence that I don't trust him and love him as I should.

Because God loves me, he rejoices when I experience his power and strength and stand up under the pressures of life for his Name's sake.

Because God loves me, he keeps on working patiently with me even when I feel like giving up and can't see why he doesn't give up with me, too.

Because God loves me, he keeps on trusting me when at times I don't even trust myself.

Because God loves me, he never says, "There is no hope for you." Rather, he patiently works with me, loves me, and disciplines me in such a way that it is hard for me to understand the depth of his concern for me.

Because God loves me, he never forsakes me even though many of my friends might.[11]

BUILDING BLOCK #5:

Learn to accept yourself.

Learn to be your own best friend by learning how to love, affirm, and support yourself.

Do you have a best friend? If so, think about your relationship with her. If not, think about what kind of relationship you'd like to have with such a person. What does a best friend provide that's so valuable—and how can you provide that for yourself?

A best friend won't condemn you. A best friend is someone to whom you can tell your worst thoughts and know you won't be judged.

A best friend will offer honest feedback. Who knows you better than you know yourself? Then why let yourself be floored by the critical comments of those who hardly know you?

A best friend will support you. You need to encourage yourself—just as your best friend would.

A best friend will hold you accountable. Just as you might tactfully and lovingly confront a best friend about a dangerous activity, so you must take a critical look at yourself from time to time. You need to know your weaknesses and work toward self-improvement.

A best friend will laugh with you. When a person laughs easily, she can usually take stressful and self-defeating situations in stride. Laughing at yourself shows you understand your own weaknesses.[12]

BUILDING BLOCK #6:

Watch TV with your child.

Watch "Mr. Rogers" on television with your children, and listen to the message as he sings his famous song:

I Like You Just the Way You Are

© 1970, Fred M. Rogers,
Used by permission.

It's you I like—every part of you—
Your skin, your eyes, your feelings, whether old or new
I hope that you'll remember
Even when you're feeling blue
That it's you I like, it's you yourself, it's you,
It's you I like.

BUILDING BLOCK #7:

Pray.

Repeat this prayer of acceptance:

Today, O Lord, I accept your acceptance of me.
I confess that you are always with me and always for me.
I receive into my spirit your grace, your mercy, your care.
I rest in your love, O Lord, I rest in your love. Amen.[13]

BUILDING BLOCK #8:

Recognize when you need help.

In taking these steps toward self-acceptance, some people bog down in the negative messages of their past and need more help than a husband or relative or friend can offer. Here are some warning signals that—if they persist—might mean you should turn to a pastor or professional counselor for help:

Loss of pleasure in life
Sleeplessness
Difficulty concentrating
Feeling of worthlessness or guilt
Low energy
Change in appetite or weight
Nervousness

FOR FURTHER READING:

The Art of Understanding Yourself, Cecil Osborne
The Art of Learning to Love Yourself, Cecil Osborne
Being a Wild Wonderful Woman for God, Becky Tirabassi
Learning to Let Go, Carol Kuykendall
My Mother, My Daughter, Elaine K. McEwan
The Pursuit of Happiness: A Woman's Search for Identity,
    Florence Littauer

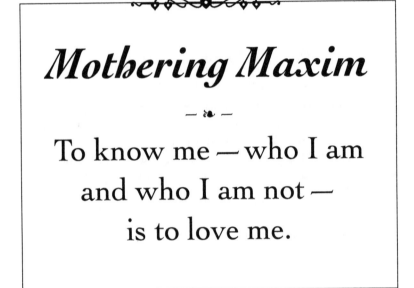

Mothering Maxim

— ❧ —

To know me — who I am
and who I am not —
is to love me.

Growth:

Sometimes I long to develop who I am

Sheila closed the baby's door and tiptoed down the hall toward the kitchen. The muscles in the back of her neck felt tense. She raised her hand to massage them as she stood, contemplating her choices.

She had an hour. Maybe an hour and a half. Amanda had been invited home with a friend after preschool. And after an active morning, Josh should sleep awhile. At thirteen months, he was into everything. Just this morning, while she was talking on the telephone, he'd committed his own version of "breaking and entering." Somehow he'd negotiated the childproof knob on the pantry, climbed up one shelf, and sprinkled a package of rice all over the pantry shelves and the kitchen floor. The cleanup had taken most of her morning.

Don't think about that now, Sheila scolded herself. *You've only got an hour, so use it.*

What she really wanted to do was to play the piano. Sheila had been a piano major in college and had taught music at the high school level for several years before Amanda was born. Even after Amanda's birth—for a couple of years, at least—she'd been able to squeeze in a few neighborhood piano lessons during afternoon naptime. Then Amanda gave up her naps. And Sheila became pregnant with Josh and just didn't have the energy. These days she barely had time to sit down at all.

Chopin called to her from the upright in the family room. Favorite nocturnes played through her head, and she entered into a familiar tug-of-war. There was a load of wash to do before Amanda returned. And she really should start dinner—the process was so much easier without Josh around. After that . . . well, forget it.

Brahms beckoned her. She wavered. No. This was not the time to succumb. She needed to make out a grocery list . . . and change the kitty litter, another impossible task with Josh "helping." In fact, she really should do that first.

As she passed by the piano, however, Mozart moved her to sit down. *Well, just for a few minutes,* she rationalized. As she perched on the bench, she touched the ivory keys, then lifted her hands and played, immediately becoming lost in the music. For fifteen whole minutes, her fingers searched out the notes on the keyboard, stroking it with a rusty grace. At times, her fingers played easily. In other sections they stumbled, but still she played, building toward a loud crescendo.

Stilled now, her hands buzzed with warm vibrations. She knew she should be playing like this every day! Otherwise, she'd lose her touch. Oh, how she longed for the freedom she once had to play and play and play. She had dreamed of obtaining a faculty position at the junior college in town. Could that dream still come true? Or would it become only a memory that grew fainter with the years?

She paused, thinking, and then heard Josh's cries echoing down the hall. Actually, they were wails. Her playing had awakened him. And she hadn't even heard him. Now he sounded scared.

How stupid of me, she thought as she slammed the cover down over the keyboard and headed down the hall. *Now I'll never get anything done this afternoon! I shouldn't have played the piano.*

LIFE LIVED ON HOLD

In this season of life, moms often make time for everyone and everything except themselves. We tend to assume that babies, toddlers, and husbands can't wait for attention, but *we can.* So we put our dreams and development on hold. And sometimes we get stuck in the distraction of the demands made upon us.

Some moms describe this stuckness as "mind mush." Where once we may have carried on intellectually stimulating dialogues, we now feel that our brains are turning to mush. We even fear we may lose the ability to think altogether!

Others get stuck in the midst of constant baby talk, which can be embarrassing when it slips out in adult company. Some moms expressed their frustration this way:

> *I forget how to talk in grown-up language. The other day I told a girlfriend to look at the moo-moos.*
>
> — 🙖 —
>
> *I never get to finish a sentence, so I rarely speak in full sentences anymore.*
>
> — 🙖 —
>
> *All I talk about these days is potty-this and potty-that.*

Still other mothers bemoan the "shelving" of parts of their personhood.

As stated in earlier chapters, mothers of preschoolers need significance, to know that their doing—their mothering—matters. They also need a sense of identity—to know who they are and to be that person with confidence.

THE NEED TO GROW

The third need we experience as mothers of young children is the need to grow and develop ourselves, both in what we do and in who we are. We have a built-in longing for self-improvement, whether that means nurturing a dream or developing more patience.

Though we enjoy investing ourselves in our families, we periodically yearn to reach and change and try and experiment and experience

> *Before I had children I spent a lot of time doing needlework. But after my second was born, I had to force myself to finish his birth sampler. I felt that my creative side was being drowned in a sea of practicality.*
>
> — 🙖 —
>
> *My husband asked what my hobbies were and I couldn't give him an answer, other than being a mom and wife. I laid everything aside when we had our daughter.*

other parts of our being. To paint! To read! To think! To create! To converse! To help another! Ah . . . to dream!

SEASON OF SELF-SACRIFICE

Mothering, by its very nature, requires self-sacrifice. This is a season when self–fulfillment naturally conflicts with self-sacrifice. Besides, we all know that, out of necessity, self–sacrifice usually wins. For most, this process begins with pregnancy when the comfort and shape of the body are compromised. Emotions spin out of control. Feet swell. Abdomens distend. Blood pressure increases.

Dream? Ha! Are you joking? Who has the time or energy?

And then at last—D-day—when the mother gives up her modesty as the baby squeezes through the birth canal, a passageway ten times smaller than it seems it should be. One woman described delivery as the process of pushing a bowling ball out one nostril. Another said it is like taking your lower lip and stretching it up over your forehead.

For those who have become mothers through adoption, the sacrifice is of the heart rather than the body. Waiting for a child can be lengthy and unpredictable. And then there is the disappointment of not being part of the birth process.

Mother and author Dale Hanson Bourke, in her book, *Everyday Miracles*, warns a mother-to-be about the emotional sacrifices of mothering: "I want her to know what she will never learn in childbirth classes: that the physical wounds of childbearing will heal, but becoming a mother will leave an emotional wound so raw that she will be forever vulnerable . . . that she will never read a newspaper again without asking, 'What if that had been my child?' That every plane crash, every fire will haunt her."[1]

While mothering young children, we learn plenty about giving up time and sleep. As we bathe wobbly, wrinkly babies, spoon sloppy cereal into mouths more interested in making bubbles, train resistant toddlers in the meaning of no, patiently watch chubby fingers master shoelaces, and then guide them as they learn to print the letters of their names—we come to know that mothering well means investing in the lives of people other than ourselves.

Love is expensive. And our children are well-served by mothers who are willing to give—and give *up*—freely. But mothering well doesn't require us to shelve our personal needs completely. Moms, too, have a legitimate need to grow as individuals, to develop their talents and abilities (doing) as well as to strengthen their character (being).

Here are some reasons why growth can't wait until later.

You need to develop yourself.

Today represents an important season in your life. You can't skip it or ignore it. And you can't ignore or neglect yourself in this season or you may find a gaping hole in the next.

You probably have dreams and desires that need to be expressed. You may have creative juices that require an outlet of expression. The "you" that has been growing since your own birth doesn't cease to exist because you've given birth to another.

I knew I wanted to be a mother and take that job seriously. But at the same time, I knew I had to cultivate my own potential in areas outside of mothering.

— ❧ —

I'm a good mother, but I don't want to discover someday that my kids are grown and I have nothing else in my life.

— ❧ —

I need to know my individuality has not been totally sacrificed to be a mother.

Your family needs you to develop yourself.

Every member of your family will benefit from the you that you are becoming.

Your family will also benefit from the wholeness of your example. They need the challenge and inspiration of your growth in order to grow themselves.

While at times it might seem that investing in yourself is an abandonment of others in your life, the truth is that when you invest in your own growth, you are more able to influence the growth of those around you. They learn to take care of themselves as they see you balancing the need to care for others as well as for yourself.

The fantasy is that your child is all you need. That your life is your child. But reality is showing me that to be a good mom, I also have to develop some other interests.

Your world needs you to develop yourself.

All around you are those who need what you have to offer. Whether it is something you do or just a natural outgrowth of the person you are, your contribution to the lives of others is increased when you develop yourself. Seeing you interact with confidence, using innate gifts and learned skills, will encourage others to discover ways in which they can improve their own lives and relationships. You may not think it is worth much, but to someone who is watching, your example is valuable.

God desires our growth.

Above all, it is God's plan for us to grow. "God loves us where we are, but he loves us too much to leave us there," reads a popular wall hanging. The Bible directs us to "grow in grace and knowledge" (2 Peter 3:18). In fact, the goal of the Christian life is to develop such Christlike qualities as love, joy, peace, patience, kindness, and goodness; the mothering season of life offers fertile soil for all of these. Yet growth doesn't come without a struggle.

GROWING PAINS

As exciting and fulfilling as developing our potential might be, it is also painful. Growing hurts. It stretches us in new directions. It uses muscles, both mental and emotional, which may have atrophied from lack of use. It demands risks that may leave us feeling vulnerable and exposed.

Change is often both inconvenient and uncomfortable. Suppose you determine you will (finally) take on a position of leadership in your church or your neighborhood and then discover that you get very nervous when speaking in front of even a small gathering. Will you agree to fulfill the commitment you made . . . or quit? If you stick it out, you'll have some stretching to do. You'll have to learn to major on your strengths and delegate to others the areas in which you are lacking.

The decision to grow is often accompanied by pain when change comes. Several realizations may hit you hard.

Growth is slow.

It takes time to grow. In the stage of life when our young children are growing like weeds, personal growth can seem tortoise-like. Life unfolds in slow motion. Like an instant replay in sports, each event unwinds in torturous tediousness, often replaying through the day.

One day on *Sesame Street*, Telly Monster was stretching and groaning when a friend of his walked by.

"Whatcha doing?" the friend asked Telly.

"I'm trying to grow!" Telly grunted as he strained his body upward and jumped a small jump.

His friend laughed. "Ha! Don'tcha know that growing takes time?"

This truth seems as surprising to us as it was to Telly Monster. Growth takes time.

Growth is hard to measure.

There are many hectic days when you can hardly tell if you're growing or shrinking. You can stand your three-year-old against the wall and see tangible evidence of his growth by marking a spot two inches above the measurement made last year. But you look at your own life, and all you can see growing is the hair on your legs!

The intangibility of the growth of character makes sticking with our goals seem discouraging. Infants don't praise us when we master patience or excellence in child care. And when we go to the wall to mark our progress, the results of our efforts may not even be noticeable.

Growth is costly.

Whether developing dreams or character, growth will cost us something.

If you're working on your piano technique or earning credit toward a college degree, you can expect to make some tough choices. Like the choice to read a book during your child's naptime and then to serve store-bought frozen dinners instead of a homemade meal. Or if you're wrestling with humility or learning how to be more assertive, you'll have to choose to admit when you're wrong or stand up for yourself when you're right.

Along with making costly choices comes the reality of accepting the consequences for these choices. Your husband may be disappointed with frozen macaroni and cheese for dinner and may communicate his displeasure in no uncertain terms. Or when you realize you've been wrong in a relationship, you'll have to apologize. Or if you're struggling with assertiveness, there will be times when you'll have to take an uncomfortable stand.

In his book, *The Pursuit of Excellence,* Ted Engstrom writes,

> Every truly worthwhile achievement of excellence has a price tag. The question you must answer for yourself is, How much am I willing to pay in hard work, patience, sacrifice and endurance to be a person of excellence?[2]

Slow, hard to measure, costly—growth often brings pain along with its rewards.

DREAMING DREAMS

So? Dreams make the difference between living a life and really *living* a life. But some of us, caught up in the busyness of childrearing, have forgotten how to dream. Here are some suggestions:

Dare to dream.

Identify where you want to grow and then start dreaming about possibilities for getting there. One writer comments, "We must dream, because we are made in the image of him who sees things that are not and wills them to be."[3]

Find a quiet spot. Sit back and let your thoughts roam. What has God already done in your life? What might he still do? Consider, just for a moment, what isn't but could be. Dream beyond where you are.

Dreams begin with asking such questions as, "If you could do anything you wanted with an extra hour today, what would it be?" Sometimes dreams have their roots in the past. "When you think back over your childhood, what did you do with your spare time?" Dreams also peer around the corners of our lives and right into the places where we live for clues as to how we can grow.

If you have trouble identifying the growth spots in your life, check the Building Blocks section at the end of this chapter. As Barbara Sher encourages in her book *Wishcraft,* the important thing is to find what you love. "There may be several things . . . whatever they are—guitar music, bridges, bird-watching, sewing, the stock market, the history of India—there is a very, very good reason why you love them. Each one is a clue to something inside you: a talent, an ability, a way of seeing the world that is uniquely yours."[4]

Identify where you want to grow. Then start dreaming a dream for your life and make a plan. A thirty-three-year-old man, recently named to a head coaching position at a major university, deflected questions about being so young for such an important position. "My parents taught me to dream with my feet on the ground. That means I dreamed about where I wanted to go and then made a plan about how to get there."

Sequence your dreams.

Once you've settled on an area of potential growth, break it down into small sections. We all know that the years of mothering young children are packed full with responsibilities and urgent tasks. If we set out to accomplish gargantuan achievements during these years, we'll probably be disappointed, because something will suffer—our children, our marriages, our dreams, or our health.

You've probably heard analogies about life being like a book, with each stage of development occupying its own chapter. During your early life, you eagerly scribbled out your contribution on the clean pages of the first few chapters. But with the arrival of children, your own journaling has been put on hold, while you help your child hold his crayon, poised and learning to write in his book of days.

I used to sit in the park with my baby and wonder what had happened to art, music, and politics. I felt isolated from the life I'd known for twenty years, so I decided to do something about it. One day I put my baby in the backpack and went to a show on impressionistic art at the museum.

Rather than setting your own journal completely aside for these next few years of childrearing, why not carefully slot time to record a few paragraphs—perhaps a single page or even a whole chapter? We can make progress toward our dreams a little at a time.

This idea of outlining life in chapters—breaking it down into sections—is sometimes called sequencing. This means giving priority to children when they are young. Then, as they grow up, we have more time for other pursuits, including the development of our dreams.

Tell someone else about your dream.

Everyone needs a nudger—someone to champion their dreams, someone to encourage them to keep dreaming when they're not sure they can. One mother describes the importance of having such friends when her circumstances forced her to give up a dream:

> Music had always been in my life. I played several instruments in various groups. In my late twenties I developed MS, which made it impossible to play and perform. Through the encouragement of friends, I discovered I have other talents, especially singing.

Dottie McDowell, wife of Josh McDowell, describes her mother as a dream-nudger who always valued what Dottie valued: "As an adult, she still dreams my dreams, wanting to know every detail and delighting in every interest that I pursue. Does this communicate that my dreams and goals have significance? You bet it does! Has that had a positive impact on my self–image—even as an adult? Of course."[5]

Maybe you have a good friend who is also dreaming while mothering. Maybe your husband knows the gifts within you and longs with you for them to be developed. Maybe your mother or aunt or sister remembers your dream and will remind you of your personal potential. Seek a nudger in your life who can help to keep your dream alive.

GET GROWING!

We were created by God to grow and change and develop. We all have great, untapped potential. As William James once observed: "Compared with what we ought to be, we are only half awake. Our fires are damped, our drafts are checked. We are making use of only a small part of our possible mental and physical resources."

So choose some Building Blocks, and nurture your need to grow. ❧

BUILDING BLOCKS

BUILDING BLOCK #1:

Find a dream!

If you don't have a dream, here are some questions and ideas to help you identify an area of passion and potential in your life:

- Is there a subject that always sparked your interest?
- What did you daydream about as a child?
- List ten positive personal characteristics. Do these traits suggest any talents or skills worth pursuing? Ask a friend to add to the list.
- Write down twenty-five things you want to do before you die. Narrow the list to ten, then five. Then rank in order of importance.[6]

BUILDING BLOCK #2:

Sample your dreams.

I'd like to . . .

- Play the piano.
- Raise golden retrievers.
- Be an Olympic medalist.
- Open a boutique.
- Start a cake decoration business at home.
- Design children's clothes.
- Write a book.
- Become a professional photographer.
- Be a clown at children's birthday parties.
- List your own possibilities:

_____

_____

_____

BUILDING BLOCK #3:

Work at home.

If your dreaming leads you toward a money-making venture, consider joining the ranks of mothers who work at home, both out of necessity and a desire to develop their skills. Do you wonder if you are cut out for the challenge? Admittedly, success demands self-discipline and the art of self-starting. Here are some self-examining questions to help you decide:

- What God-given skills and talents can I channel into a home-based job?
- Where can I situate my workplace? One woman remodeled her garage, another set up an office in the walk-in closet of her guest bedroom. Or you might be able to claim a corner of your family room.
- How saturated is the market I want to enter? The local chamber of commerce or a phone book's Yellow Pages can give clues. So can an informal survey of how they are doing. If already established businesses seem to have more customers than they can handle, there probably is room for competition.[7]

BUILDING BLOCK #4:

Build your character.

Are you hoping for more patience, self-discipline, or perseverance? Here are two resources:

- Try "Life Mapping," a process described in John Trent's book by the same name. Life Mapping is a solution-oriented process that seeks to uncover a person's God-given strengths. While it encourages a person to gain insight from her past, it's based on setting clear goals and plans with a strong hope for the future. Trent remarks, "It holds the promise of moving away from negative patterns and toward the intimacy, purpose and direction you've always wanted."[8]

- Read to your children from William J. Bennett's collection, *The Book of Virtues*, filled with great stories about ten character qualities that will help us learn alongside our children. As the author explains, "The vast majority of Americans share a respect for certain fundamental traits of character: honesty, compassion, courage, and perseverance. These are virtues. But because children are not born with this knowledge, they need to learn what true virtues are.[9]

BUILDING BLOCK #5:

Find a nudger.

A nudger is a person who encourages you to dream and then to act on your dreams.

- Do you have a nudger in your life?
- Identify three people who have served as nudgers in your past. How did they specifically nudge you?
- What qualities would you look for in a nudger?
- List three possible nudgers you might cultivate in your future.

BUILDING BLOCK #6:

Make a "dreamcatcher."

Tangible symbols remind us of those things we hold dear, or give us targets to aim at. A seashell picked up on a summer beach vacation and set on a writing desk recalls a time of walking and wondering in solitude. A smooth rock from a mountain stream found while fishing and kept on the mantel reminds us of how the rushing waters of life polish the wrinkles in our souls. A refrigerator magnet of an artist's easel and brush offers daily encouragement that God, who began a good work in us, is not finished with us yet. "He who began a good work in you will carry it on to completion until the day of Christ Jesus" (Phil. 1:6). We are his masterpieces in the making. We are in process.

- Choose some symbols that will remind you to keep your dream alive and growing. Conrad Hilton, when rebuilding his small hotel chain after the Depression, kept a picture of the grand Waldorf Hotel on his desk. A young mother, aspiring to be a writer someday, kept a writer's quill in her kitchen as a symbol of her dream.
- Select a spot to hold reminders. A place on your nightstand. A bookshelf. A space on the refrigerator door.
- Be on the lookout for symbols to add to your collection. Pause to enjoy them periodically to remind yourself of your growth choices in your life, the embers of dreams that you know will be kindled into flames in the future.

BUILDING BLOCK #7:

Be inspired.

Louise Driscoll encourages us to hang in there in her poem, "Hold Fast Your Dream":

> Hold fast your dream!
> Within your heart
> Keep one still secret spot
> Where dreams may go,
> And sheltered so,
> May thrive and grow—
> Where doubt and fear are not.
> Oh, keep a place apart
> Within your heart,
> For little dreams to go.[10]

As Brenda Hunter writes, "When God gives you a dream, he will help you to realize it. It may take a year or half a lifetime, but God planted that dream in your consciousness for a reason. God and you will make dreams become realities."[11]

BUILDING BLOCK #8:

Read a book.

Choose a book from the recommended reading list and talk about it with a friend.

FOR FURTHER READING:

At-Home Motherhood: Making It Work for You, Cindy Tolliver
The Book of Virtues, William J. Bennett
Emotional Phases of a Woman's Life, Jean Lush
Homemade Business, Donna Partow
In His Steps, Charles Sheldon
Life Mapping, John Trent
My Utmost for His Highest, Oswald Chambers
What Color Is Your Parachute? Richard Bolles
Wishcraft, Barbara Sher with Annie Gottlieb
Work At Home Options, Joanne Cleaver

Mothering Maxim

— ❧ —

What I am is God's gift
to me. What I become
is my gift to God.

Four

Intimacy:
Sometimes I long to be understood

Five-thirty. Dinnertime. Well, at least she'd made it this far. She opened the refrigerator and surveyed the boring contents. *It's so hard to cook for just me and the kids,* she thought. *I hate it when Paul is out of town.* But then, it was more than dinnertime that made Barb miss Paul.

Making a quick decision, she called to Nathan and Kelli, "Hey, kids! We're going to McDonald's!" Whoops and hollers preceded their wild dash for the car. Barb gathered up little Emily in her infant seat, grabbed her purse, and followed.

The parking lot was crowded, so she cautioned Nathan and Kelli to hold hands and walk in front of her. In line, Barb held the infant seat and gently guided the other two until they reached the front, where she ordered Happy Meals® all around.

They all slid into a booth, and Barb placed Emily, still strapped into her seat, next to her. Then Barb began the task of squeezing out catsup, securing crooked lids on drinks, and pushing napkins at greasy fingers.

Nathan and Kelli downed three-quarters of their burgers and fries and begged to go to the play area. Since she could keep an eye on them through the window near the booth, Barb agreed.

Glancing around the crowded room, she saw—in the booth diagonal to hers—a young mom and dad holding hands while smiling at their chubby-faced toddler. One table down was a group of loud teenagers, cocky and oblivious to all around them. Behind her, another mom appeared to be in deep conversation with her preteen daughter. Everyone she saw seemed content and connected to someone.

Barb felt a familiar longing. Loneliness. It seemed absurd. How could she sit in this room filled with people and feel alone? How could she *ever* feel lonely with three children around every minute?

She looked outside. Nathan and Kelli were playing happily. Emily had dozed off in her infant seat. Barb sighed and idly played with her straw. With her index finger, she plugged the top of the straw, then lifted it from her Diet Coke® and let the liquid trickle out. People came and went through the restaurant doors. Meanwhile, her loneliness lingered.

Stop! Barb scolded herself. *You have three healthy kids, a husband with a good job. Isn't that enough? It should be,* she reasoned, yet she longed for someone to talk to. Someone who would understand her fears and her struggles with contentment and patience.

Just then, a woman about her age, carrying a tray laden with three Happy Meals®, slid into the booth next to hers. Two little boys—about five and seven years old—followed. From the mother's face, Barb could tell she was a woman who loved what she was doing, even as she patiently squeezed out catsup, straightened crooked lids on drinks, and pushed napkins at greasy fingers.

When her boys ran off to the play area, the woman looked up and her eyes met Barb's. Across the cluttered table, she smiled. "So you're eating gourmet tonight, too?"

Barb laughed and suddenly she felt better. Here they were—total strangers. They would probably never see each other again. But in those few words, Barb felt understood for the first time in ages.

THAT ONE AND ONLY LONELY FEELING

Mothers of preschoolers overwhelmingly report that their greatest struggle is with loneliness, a feeling of being disconnected or isolated. Though the words may vary, the feelings describe a common need for intimacy—a longing to be understood.

Ouch! Loneliness hurts. It stings. It sucks out all the filling inside a woman and pierces the exposed, unprotected places.

Perhaps the reason loneliness hurts so much is that it blocks what we intrinsically need as humans. "The Bible proclaims our need for connection," says psychologist John Townsend in his book, *Hiding from Love.* "At the deepest spiritual and emotional level, we are beings who need safety and a sense of belonging in our three primary relationships: God, self, and others. We begin life in a terrified and disconnected state. . . . It is the deepest and most fundamental problem we can experience."[1]

Keeping up with the kids isn't the hardest part of mothering; it's the loneliness.

— ❧ —

I need someone to unload on, someone to listen to me.

— ❧ —

I need someone who understands what I'm saying even when I don't understand it myself.

In other words, our need for connection is a need created within us by God. He created us to be in relationship with others. And this need or *longing* is answered by a sense of *belonging,* which is also known as being in community. We are said to be in community when we are connected to others in some context of meaningful relationships in which we have a sense of belonging and shared sense of nurturing and being nurtured.

Loneliness is on the increase. But today's frantic lifestyle simply doesn't lend itself to being in community. Heidi Brennan, who works with a national advocacy group, Mothers at Home, remarks, "People miss the backyard fence. Even working women. Women are community people and even in the workplace, we attempt to create a sense of community."[2]

At-home mothers are critically aware of this need. Author and psychologist Brenda Hunter quotes one mom in her book, *The Company of Women:* "Since I've become a full-time mother, my friends have become very important in creating a new peer

group, a sense of community and support as I tackle the difficult task of mothering."[3]

We have this need for community—for intimacy—but before we can find it and invest in it, we have to know what it is
. . . and what it is *not*.

EXPLAINING INTIMACY

What is intimacy? The word alone evokes all kinds of images!

Isn't intimacy sex? Hugs and kisses and touching? Well . . .
yes and no. Intimacy may involve sexual expression and physical communication. But intimacy is more than sex.

Well then, isn't intimacy something like romance? Again,
the answer is yes . . . and no. Intimacy may be romantic at times.
But it doesn't have to be.

Okay. Intimacy is like having a constant companion who
knows you inside and out and likes you, warts and all. Right?
Again, yes and no. But the truth is, intimacy rarely occurs in one
relationship alone. In fact, when we depend upon only one relationship for our intimacy, we often end up strangling that partnership with too many expectations. Our healthy need for
intimacy should not be satisfied in only one place.

The Latin word for *inner* or *innermost* is *intimus*. From this
root comes our word *intimate*. Webster defines *intimate* as in-
trinsic, essential, that which characterizes one's deepest nature,
personal.

Another popular definition of the word *intimacy* takes the
meaning home to everyday life. Intimacy means "Into-me-see."
When we are intimate with someone, we allow him to see into
our character, our personhood. We become transparent and feel
safe to admit our fears and longings.

*After I had my first baby I felt that my whole outlook was
changing. I was suddenly needed for everything my little baby
did. One day everything was going wrong. My son wouldn't
have anything to do with me—I—the one who did everything
for him. I couldn't get him to eat, to stop crying. If I tried to*

hold him, he screamed and kicked at me. I called my mother, crying uncontrollably, and asked her to please come over and help me, to tell me what I was doing wrong. She managed to calm my son and me, then she just listened and nodded every now and then to everything I felt and said.

What is intimacy? To a mother of preschoolers, the definition is simple. Intimacy is being understood. It's not being judged for what you did wrong this time. It's not being told what you could do differently next time. It's not being corrected, interpreted, or "fixed." Intimacy is being understood, sometimes when you don't even understand yourself.

STUMBLING BLOCKS TO INTIMACY

Even when we recognize our need for intimacy, we find some obstacles that block our pathway to experiencing it.

I'm too tired to be friendly.

There's no arguing with the reality that moms of preschoolers have very little energy to spend on intimacy. After four nights with little sleep because of a teething, fussy six-month-old, keeping up with the constant responsibility of putting meals on the table, cleaning up, and doing laundry, few of us have energy left over for friends.

Most of my friends work, so there's no time for friendship, except at night when I'm too tired.

— ❧ —

After moving to our fourth home in four years with children ages one and four, the thought of making new friends was too overwhelming, so I just stayed at home with the kids and felt lonely.

Moms are also often too tired to even relate well to their husbands.

With the onset of parenthood, I often felt tired and put my husband in last place. I remember one particularly exhausting day when by the time we got into bed, all I wanted to do was sleep. That's not what he had in mind, but I was too tired to care.

I don't want to risk making a friend because one of us will just move away.

In our mobile society, few of us stay in one place long enough to put down the roots necessary to build intimacy. We're separated from our hometowns and the long-term relationships with people who "knew us when," and we fear that we can never be "known" again.

I don't have time to be friendly.

"Women today don't have time for friendships," says Heidi Brennan. "We're more task-oriented in the '90s than earlier, and friendship takes a lot of time."[4] And psychologist Brenda Hunter goes on to comment, "It takes fallow, kickback time to nurture relationships, and with the cultural emphasis on achievement . . . friendships with other women are the first to go."[5]

If we're employed and mothering, we let go of friendships in order to survive. If we're mothering without external employment, we often look around the neighborhood, only to find that no one else is available during the few precious daytime moments we could be free. And when a husband comes home, his needs and the needs of the children come first, ahead of intimacy with friends.

I'm uncomfortable with being friendly.

Every one of us understands the ongoing struggle to be appropriately intimate. Some of us think it might be easier and maybe even more mature to remain independent of intimate relationships. "No one has trouble understanding why Adam couldn't live alone in paradise," writes Joan Wulff, "but we somehow tell ourselves we can make it alone in today's world."[6]

Others face fear and uncertainty about responsibilities when it comes to developing relationships. As Richard Fowler observes, "Anxiety in interpersonal relationships stems not from a complete unwillingness to socialize or respond, but from confusion about what our roles should be in nurturing and developing relationships."[7]

Perhaps we've been locked into unhealthy relationships in the past and are afraid we'll repeat those old habits. Or maybe we've observed less-than-perfect models of intimacy and so wonder what exactly is normal and healthy.

Some of us even defeat ourselves, refraining from embracing the very thing we need. A newspaper article about loneliness explains: "Lonely people are more critical of themselves, more disappointed with others and less willing to take risks in social situations. They are afraid of closeness and actually talk themselves out of being connected to others. They'd rather feel depressed and alone than risk rejection."[8]

We're too tired, we live in a transient society, we don't have time, we're uncomfortable—for a number of obvious reasons, we struggle with intimacy. In her book *No More Lone Ranger Moms,* Donna Partow quotes a woman who sums up the stumbling blocks to intimacy: "I dropped out of school when I became a mom. I don't have homework. I don't have colleagues. My family is several hundred miles away and my husband works from three o'clock in the afternoon to midnight. I hardly ever see him. I was always a loner, but I never felt lonely until I became a mom."[9]

WHERE TO FIND INTIMACY

Where do we find intimacy? In a variety of places. Intimacy can happen one-on-one with a friend, week after week over coffee. It can occur in a marriage when views are exchanged and feelings are respected. Intimacy can happen in a group—in community—where feelings are shared.

Rather than taking place only in a single ultra-close connection, intimacy most likely will transpire in many exchanges over a lifetime and, sometimes, in several spots in one day. In a certain season of life, a mom might find intimacy in one particular friendship. Then in other stages, she might find it in another. Intimacy can even happen between total strangers who share a moment of understanding over Happy Meals® at McDonald's.

Before suggesting where to find intimacy, here's a word of caution about where *not* to look for it. Don't look for intimacy with your children. Sure. They're available. They have our attention, and they have our hearts. But they are not given to us to meet *our* needs; they should not feel that kind of pressure. "Children do not exist to please us," writes author and professor Walter Wangerin. "They are not for us at all, but rather we exist for them, to protect them now and prepare them for the future."[10]

There may be a time for intimacy with our children when they are adults, but moms who look to their children to meet these needs are looking in the wrong place. When we're looking for intimacy, we should look in places with appropriate potential.

Marriage

Our relationship with our life partner is the most likely, and certainly the most important, source of intimacy. It is also the most challenging. Added to the stress of caring for children is the sense that an escalating divorce rate in our society makes marriage a less-than-safe place.

Why is intimacy in marriage such a struggle? Besides the obvious stumbling blocks to intimacy—fatigue, transience, lack of time, unhealthy relational patterns—there are several unique hurdles to overcome as we work toward intimacy in marriage.

For example, men and women may interpret intimacy differently. When one partner seeks intimacy, he may be looking for companionship or sex. For the other, intimacy may mean the close connection of being understood.

In addition, babies—whether one or many—change the marriage relationship. In some ways the change is wonderful, as author Dale Hanson Bourke tells a friend contemplating motherhood: "My friend's relationship with her husband will change, but not in the ways she thinks. I wish she could understand how much more you can love a man who is always careful to powder the baby or who never hesitates to play with his son or daughter. I think she should know that she will fall in love with her husband again for reasons she would now find very unromantic."[11]

There's another response, however. The "down" side of the up-and-down-ness of adjusting to a new baby. Slowly a husband and wife realize that their communication patterns have changed. They are less intimate, more custodial.

> *My husband and I have such mechanical conversations these days, mostly about our kids and our responsibilities. "Did you mail that package? We need more dog food. What shall we do about Allison's tantrums?" The other day I asked him what he wanted for his birthday.*
>
> *"I don't know," he answered.*
>
> *"Please tell me something," I begged, "because I'm going out tomorrow afternoon and I have to get you something."*
>
> *"Don't bother," he said. "It's gotten too mechanical . . . just like everything else around here."*
>
> *And I felt really hurt.*

Another mom describes how motherhood introduced a different wrinkle in her relationship with her husband:

> *John and I have enjoyed marriage and struggled to understand what other married couples argue about vehemently. Needless to say, our honeymoon was an extended one. The day our baby arrived, we suddenly seemed to find an accumulation of differences we had no idea existed. We have to keep reminding ourselves that we are on the same team; we're in this together.*

Many moms admitted falling in love with their new babies, the kind of surprising, consuming love that sometimes closed out their husbands.

Overcoming these additional stumbling blocks to intimacy in marriage is challenging, but the challenge can be rewarding. Here are a few suggestions for establishing intimacy with your husband.

> *My husband says he feels like I love our children more than him and fear grips my heart when I realize that he might be right.*

•**Ask.** Ask your husband questions. Just a few at a time. Probing, curious questions. Interesting questions. What is his greatest dream in life? If he could do anything he chose with his time when he turns fifty, what would it be? What three adjectives would he like others to use in describing him?

Even when my baby was asleep, I had no time for my husband because one ear was always tuned to listen for her cry. I found myself worthless as a sexual partner because I couldn't stop thinking about the baby.

Ask questions you'd like to be asked. Questions that reflect your own curiosity. Questions that encourage him to be open, to share his dreams.

•**Listen.** After asking, listen. Open your ears and take in all you hear. Resist the urge to critique, redirect, evaluate. Just listen, accepting whatever you hear as having worth and value because it reflects something about the one you love.

"It is impossible to overemphasize the immense need people have to be listened to, to be taken seriously, to be understood," writes Paul Tournier. "No one can develop freely in this world and find a full life without feeling understood by at least one person."[12]

•**Act.** After asking and listening, then put what you hear into action. Did you catch that tone in his voice—the one that says he's afraid you won't take him seriously? Did you grab that chance to compliment him in front of your friends?

Establish closeness in the little things. Lock eyes and wink from across a room. Share the buzz word or a private joke. Squeeze a hand in church. Blow a kiss through the window.

•**Risk.** It's not enough only to receive the shared soul of another person. If we want to establish true intimacy with another, we must also take the risk to unveil who we are as well.

I need to be able to talk to my husband about the things that are nearest and dearest to my heart, but it is hard for me to be vulnerable and step out in faith and trust him with my emotions.

We teeter on the edge of intimacy, fearing

a free fall into its fulfillment. But to flee from risking is to forfeit intimacy altogether.

•**Adjust.** Marriages change. And they should, because the people in them change. As we invest in intimacy, we must be open to adjusting ourselves within our relationships from time to time.

> *My husband and I keep learning so much about ourselves and each other through parenthood. And we keep having to face new fears and make changes in ourselves that impact our relationship. Keeping up with each other has been pretty tough.*

•**Forgive.** Any time two people spend lots of time together, they are bound to irritate each other periodically with their quirky little habits, even those habits that seemed interesting or fun before marriage. "Opposites attract—until they get married" is a familiar saying. So we have to practice the art of forgiving. And the art of not holding grudges. "Keep short accounts," a pastor advised a soon-to-be-married couple, quoting Scripture. "Do not let the sun go down while you are still angry" (Eph. 4:26). The habit of holding onto grudges becomes a brick wall to building intimacy.

Ask. Listen. Act. Risk. Adjust. Forgive. All of these are suggestions for building intimacy with spouses. In general, the ongoing kindling of intimacy in a marriage takes time and effort and intentionality, but the effort will strengthen and protect your relationship with your mate.

But remember, seeking intimacy in marriage alone puts too much strain on the relationship. As Cecil Osborne says in his book, *The Art of Understanding Your Mate,* "There are no perfect marriages for the simple reason there are no perfect people, and no one person can satisfy all of one's needs."[13]

Don't expect your husband to meet all your needs. He can't. Moms of preschoolers, whether married, single, or separated geographically from family and friends, need the intimacy of friendship. Writer and mother Valerie Bell described this revelation recently to some MOPS members:

As a young wife and mother, I remember sitting by our front bay window, playing the "counting game" with my two small sons. It went like this: "How long do you think it will be 'til Daddy comes home? I bet if we count to fifty, he'll be here." Daddy rarely came on the first count. For the boys, it was a game. But for me—a young mom isolated with their care all day long—the number counting was not a game. Every lonely number was filled with a longing for my husband who happened to be my major link to the outside world.

Then one morning, a woman about my age showed up on my doorstep with doughnuts and her two children. Her name was Rosie.

"Let's have breakfast, let's talk, let's be friends." She was a lifeline that morning and uncountable other mornings as we shared our secrets, took comfort in the mutual naughtiness of our children, laughed and dreamed and cried and prayed together. Her friendship gave me a link to the outside world and a unique kind of connection that even my husband couldn't provide.

Friendships

One after another, moms cry out for the understanding provided uniquely through women-friends. This need started early in life. Most females remember their "first best friend" during preadolescence, a friend with whom to share secrets, write notes, and have weekend sleepovers. During teenage years, best friends start competing with boyfriends, a competition that often lasts during courtship and the first few years of marriage. But then another stage begins, when many

I have a need to find my kindred spirit, my bosom buddy. Someone who is just like me. Someone who likes to do activities with the kids and would be loving and accepting of who I am. After marrying and having children, I lost touch with all female friends and devoted myself fully to my family. I miss the one-on-one talks and camaraderie of female friends.

husbands are working hard and many moms with young children greatly need close women friends again.

We long for friendships that are deep and fulfilling because here we find the intimacy we need: We feel understood.

Even in friendships we must overcome some unique stumbling blocks. For example, we might be tempted to idealize a friend as the cure-all for our problems during these days of raising needy young ones, or we may long for the perfect friend who doesn't exist.

But just as no marriage can meet our every need for intimacy, neither can a single friendship or wished-for best friend. We must be realistic.

Another barrier to friendship is being overly possessive. At times, we find ourselves acting like a two-year-old who must first claim an object as "Mine!" before it can be shared with others, or a five-year-old who demands that a friend be her best and *only* friend. In friendship, as in marriage, possessiveness suffocates. But, unlike marriage, the mark of the most mature friendship may be the open-handedness of sharing our friends with other friends.

I have many friends and I cherish each one. But I pray to meet a friend who can be my best friend. Her husband and my husband click, our children get along. We spend time together baking, having tea, laughing together. . . .

We must also recognize that friends come and go in different seasons or arenas of life. Some friends move away. Circumstances change. One woman might have been an intimate friend in the workplace, but now that you're a mom, temporarily at home, you may have less in common. One woman recently differentiated between "friends for the road" and "friends for the heart." Not every friend is meant to be our best friend, and not every friendship is meant to be forever. "'Friends for the road' are the people God puts in our life for a short time or a specific purpose. But a friend for the heart . . . that's the friendship that's meant to last."[14]

One other piece of advice about close friends, however: When we transfer a relationship of emotional intimacy from a husband to a friend, we border on the problem of committing *emotional* adultery. For the married woman, friendships are meant to complement and complete the need for intimacy, not replace it altogether so that emotional intimacy is unnecessary or neglected in the marriage relationship.

One woman admitted that her friends in MOPS "husbanded" her through the early years of her marriage when her husband was a medical intern and largely unavailable to her. While this kind of help is comforting and meets an immediate need, it may also rob a woman of establishing that kind of intimacy with her husband.

Once we understand the possible barriers to intimacy in friendship, how can we start making close friendships? While the process of friend-making and friend-keeping is lifelong, here are some suggestions to help us along the way.

If you want a friend, be a friend.

Figure out what you value most in a friendship and then work on developing and modeling those qualities yourself.

Most people appreciate a friend who knows how to keep a confidence. If this is the most important trait to you, then respect the confidence of your friends rather than sharing them indiscriminately. Perhaps you prefer a companion who will listen without interrupting or judging. Then close your mouth and open your ears when you listen. You may want an outdoorsy type of person who enjoys fresh air and exercise. So get out there and start walking. Maybe you'll meet your friend along the hiking trail!

Seek friends on "common ground."

During this season of life, moms need other moms to share their joys and struggles. Seek friends with common circumstances, such as other mothers of young children or other moms with "special needs" children. Look for support groups that meet your unique needs. MOPS is the perfect example. This organization, designed for mothers of preschoolers, meets in churches all around the country. Call a local church or the International Headquarters of MOPS (303–733–5353) to find out about the availability of a group in your area.

Open yourself to unexpected friendships.

If a person of another culture, another faith, another generation, or another background lands in your life, you'll have an opportunity to make an unexpected friendship. Such a situation might present certain challenges—stretching or adjusting our attitudes—but these special friendships can enlarge and encourage as well.

In the Building Blocks section of this chapter, you'll find more suggestions for identifying sources of intimacy in your life. Whether in marriage or in friendship, we have a built-in longing for closeness. Moms need to be understood. When we understand that need and move to meet it appropriately, we'll be more prepared to be the moms we want to be for our children. ❧

BUILDING BLOCKS

M **BUILDING BLOCK #1:**

Increase intimacy in your marriage.

Answering these questions will help you increase the level of intimacy in your marriage:

1. True or False: I maintain an active interest in my husband's work and make an effort to keep up with the names, problems, and office politics he shares with me.
2. True or False: My husband and I have made our marriage a priority above our relationship with our children.
3. True or False: We spend time alone each week.
4. True or False: My husband and I openly discuss our feelings about house rules for the children, spending, housework, and standards and values.
5. Think back to when you were dating. What sorts of things did you do then that you would like to do more of now? Write down three activities you could reinstate in your relationship.

   _____
   _____
   _____

6. When do you and your husband talk the most? (In the car, when you're out for dinner, after the kids go to bed?) Build in those situations and consciously use that time for talking.

   _____
   _____
   _____

7. List three things you could do to help your husband get more enjoyment out of his new role.

   _____

   _____

   _____

8. List three little things you could do to improve the quality of the time you and your husband spend together.

   _____

   _____

   _____

9. How do you and your husband split up household and parenting responsibilities? Are you happy with this arrangement? What would you like to change?

   _____

   _____

   _____

10. What unrealistic expectations about marriage and parenting do you have, if any?

    _____

    _____

    _____

11. What do you think are your husband's three biggest worries? Ask him, and see if you were right.

    _____

    _____

    _____

12. What do you think are your three biggest strengths as a wife? Ask your husband what he thinks they are, and compare. Conversely, decide what your husband's three greatest strengths are as a husband. Ask him what he thinks they are and once again, compare.[15]

    _____

    _____

    _____

BUILDING BLOCK #2:

Learn the difference between romance and real love.

For generations, people have attempted to describe the difference between romance and love. Author Marjorie Holmes offers the following subtle—yet important—distinctions:

> *Romance* is seeking perfection. . . . *Love* is forgiving faults.
>
> *Romance* is fleeting. . . . *Love* is long.
>
> *Romance* is flying. . . . *Love* is a safe landing.
>
> *Romance* is the anguish of waiting for the phone to ring to bring you a voice that will utter endearments. . . . *Love* is the anguish of waiting for a call that will assure you someone else is happy and safe.
>
> *Romance* is eager, striving always to appear attractive to each other. . . . *Love* is two people who find beauty in each other no matter how they look.
>
> *Romance* is dancing in the moonlight, gazing deep into desired eyes across a candlelit table. . . . *Love* is saying, "You're tired, honey, I'll get up this time," and stumbling through the darkness to warm a bottle or comfort a frightened child.[16]

BUILDING BLOCK #3:

Develop friendships and nurture them.

- Don't feel guilty taking time for socializing. It's not a waste of time. You need this interaction. If you have come home from a career, think of it as part of your job to create the perks for yourself that were already built in for you when you worked outside the home.
- Volunteer. The more you do in your community, the greater your chances for meeting people. Sharing work promotes good conversation and mutual respect. This is often the best route for a truly shy person.

- Integrate your daily errands or exercise routines with social time with friends. For example, if you have to make a big haul at a discount food club, plan to go with your friend. Arrange for your and your friend's child to take ballet or swim lessons at the same time. Get a long cord or a cordless phone so you can visit with a friend while you fold laundry, unload the dishwasher, or perform other "mindless" chores.
- Be a special events organizer. Everyone loves to participate, but not everyone will take the time to make the arrangements. If you plan to attend a lecture series or a children's play, ask a friend to join you. Scan the entertainment section for details about special events of interest to mothers and their children and put together a group. If the weather's nice, call two or three mothers and ask them to meet you for a picnic in the park. Organize a discussion group for at-home mothers.
- Be positive. This sounds trite, but it's basic to making and keeping friends. We are attracted to friends who bring out the best, most treasured parts of ourselves. We drive people away with chronic complaining or harsh criticism of others. On the other hand, if you're happy doing what you're doing and show it, others will enjoy your company.
- Expect the ebb and flow of friendship. We all need to pull back sometimes to allow ourselves or a friend some space.
- If a friendship is in trouble, analyze the cause. Apologize if you have hurt someone. If your friend has hurt you, let her know how you feel as clearly and lovingly as you can. If your friend has let you down in some way, remember that part of friendship is forgiving shortcomings. Sometimes we may strongly and persistently disapprove of a friend's actions. If the relationship can bear it, offer suggestions and hope the situation turns around. But if you see that she continues to create chaos in her own life

or in others' lives through her actions, your ambivalent feelings may force you to withdraw from the relationship.

- Don't be afraid to request favors of your friends. In creating obligations to one another we bond more deeply. Ben Franklin's advice to be neither borrower nor lender doesn't hold true here as long as you return favors and borrowed goods in good shape and within reasonable amounts of time.

- Don't join the so-called "mommy wars" between mothers who work outside the home and at-home mothers. We need each other too much and have too much in common to regard each other as enemies. Can you remain friends with your working friends? Of course. As long as you keep up other interests besides curing the baby's diaper rash or keeping the carpets clean, you'll find plenty to talk about. Your self-confidence is the biggest factor in how you relate to working women. If you're insecure about the value of your job at home, you may find time spent with former work friends distressing rather than rejuvenating. Bear in mind that many women's jobs are not glamorous, stimulating, or well-paid. They probably envy your freedom.

- Don't let treasured friends drift away. If you both like basketball games or the theater, buy season tickets so you can sit together. Make a standing monthly date for lunch or dinner. Getting it on the calendar ups the chances for making it happen.

- Keep this oldie but goodie in mind: "You've got to be a friend to have a friend." Try to find ways to bring joy into friends' lives. Be available when your friends need you. When you're together, listen supportively and nonjudgmentally. When your friend has a problem, try to guide her to her own conclusions. If necessary, help her find help. Don't be afraid to open up to your friends: Social facades are boring; the truth never is.[17]

BUILDING BLOCK #4:

Follow these do's and don'ts of building friendships.

DO

Reexamine the people in your life. There just might be a bosom buddy hiding among your family members or acquaintances. If not, venture out and become active in a club, church group, or social cause.

Be encouraging. Honesty is the best policy, but criticism can also be crushing. If your opinion is going to hurt a fledgling relationship, don't voice it. There's a lot to be said for diplomacy.

Stay away from gossip. Proverbs 11:13 says, "A gossip betrays a confidence, but a trustworthy man keeps a secret." It's easy to pass on our opinions about others. But your friend will reason, "If she talks about them behind their backs, then she's liable to do the same behind mine."

Schedule your visits. Just as it's important to your physical health to squeeze in exercise, you need to make time for friends for your emotional health.

Be spontaneous. Call a new friend on the spur of the moment to see how she's doing and remind her that you care. It can be a cold world out there. A little warmth will be a welcome change.

DON'T

Don't assume your new friend feels the same as you. When you call, ask if it's a good time to talk before diving into conversation. And when you get together, sense her mood. If it's negative, don't take it personally. She could be reacting to something else or simply needs a listening ear.

Don't talk about yourself first—unless asked to. Naturally there are exceptions, but try to recognize someone's need to unload what's on her mind. Satisfy her first, and she'll be more likely to give you her undivided attention later.

Don't spend all your time together. You can have too much of a good thing. So it is with friends. After a while, you'll get on each other's nerves. Go your own way for a short time, and you'll find yourself refreshed and your appreciation of each other renewed.

Don't think you have to have a lot in common. Broaden your horizons. Some of the spiciest friendships contain opposite personalities. A friend with different interests can broaden your perspective or introduce you to new activities.[18]

BUILDING BLOCK #5:

Try these when you're lonely.

Take the initiative in one or more of the following ways whenever you're feeling lonely:

- Call someone.
- Get physical. Take a walk. Clean a room.
- Be quiet. Turn loneliness into solitude with stillness.
- Be positive. Fight off the downward spiral of negativity. Count up your blessings.
- Write an encouraging note to someone else.
- Be involved. The best cure for the need for intimacy is to be a friend to someone else.

BUILDING BLOCK #6:

Let Jesus be your Friend.

Be comforted and directed by these words written by Sister Basilea Schink:

> "The Lord in his love has planned pathways of loneliness for us, not so that our hearts will be tormented or embittered, but so that we shall seek him and draw closer to him."[19]

BUILDING BLOCK #7:

Memorize an inspirational quotation.

A friend is a present you give yourself.
>   —Robert Louis Stevenson

When we glimpse a reflection of ourselves in the soul of another, that is the beginning of friendship.
>   —Pauline R. Pritchard

Friendships are discovered rather than made.
>   —Harriet Beecher Stowe

A good friend overlooks your broken-down gate and admires the flowers in your window.
>   —Anonymous

Friends—they are kind to each other's hopes. They cherish each other's dreams.
>   —Henry David Thoreau

Inside us all, there are places only a friend can reach.
>   —Michele Bryson

Wishing to be friends is quick work, but friendship is a slow-ripening fruit.
>   —Aristotle

FOR FURTHER READING:

The Friendship Factor, Alan McInnis
The Friendships of Women, Dee Brestin
Hedges: Loving Your Marriage Enough to Protect It, Jerry Jenkins
Holding Onto Romance, H. Norman Wright
Home Remedies: Timeless Prescriptions for Today's Family, Gary Smalley
    and John Trent
In the Company of Women, by Brenda Hunter
Love for a Lifetime, Dr. James Dobson
Still the One, Jerry Jenkins
Strike the Original Match, Charles Swindoll
Traits of a Lasting Marriage, Jim and Sally Conway

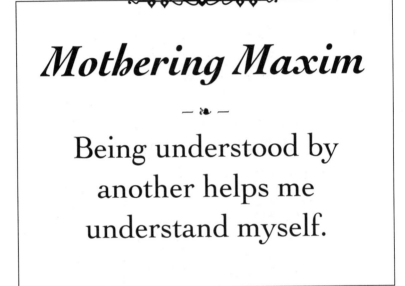

Mothering Maxim

— ❧ —

Being understood by
another helps me
understand myself.

Instruction:

Sometimes I don't know what to do

"*N*o! I don't wanna sit at the table, and you can't make me!*" screeched three-year-old Benjamin.

Ruthie shot her husband David a look of panic across the table. Benjamin was about to throw a tantrum right here in front of her in-laws and all of David's brothers and sisters and their perfectly behaved children. And she didn't have a clue as to what to do about it.

"He's tired." She smiled weakly, searching for some excuse for her child's poor behavior. "After all, we've been riding in the car for nearly eight hours."

At that moment, David grabbed Benjamin and tried to force him into his seat at the table. Ruthie could see the tension in her husband's face.

"*Daddy! Let go of my arm! Mommy! I want Mommy!*" Benjamin wailed.

Ruthie reached out for him, but he swung away and ran screaming toward the kitchen. Both Ruthie and David dashed after him while all the relatives watched. Without even looking, Ruthie could feel the judgment on their faces.

"Ruthie!" David hissed over his shoulder as he caught the child. "I told you we shouldn't have given him that Coke® at the gas station. Now he's all wired, and he'll never settle down!"

Ruthie's forced smile was in place. But beneath the plastic mask, she was churning—against David, against Benjamin, against marriage and three-year-olds and visits to in-laws and decisions like whether or not to give toddlers a Coke® or a spanking or a "time out" . . . or what.

How was she supposed to know, anyway? She'd never been a mom before, and her own family had done things so differently. Not that she really wanted to model herself after them, either—at least, not exactly.

Suddenly, she was very tired of all these questions with no clear answers. Life used to be so much simpler before she became a mother. So many times now she just didn't know what to do!

WHAT'S A MOTHER TO DO?

When a woman becomes a mother, she enters foreign territory. We may have observed our own mothers mothering, our grandmothers mothering, a good friend mothering, or even a woman in front of us in line at the grocery store mothering. But we come into mothering ignorant of what it means to mother our own children. Not only that, but during the earliest stages of mothering, we also lack information on what marriage should look like, how to manage our time with so many other lives dependent upon ours, how to stay on top of our finances, and how to understand our value and identity as women and mothers.

I was given the position of mothering without a training manual. I went from the corporate world to being a full-time mom and needed help making this transition. In the working world, I always felt confident and in control, but motherhood opened up a world of uncertainty where I realized I had much to learn.

When we become mothers, we ask the perennial question of motherhood: What's a mother to do?

QUESTIONS, QUESTIONS, QUESTIONS

The expressions of need come from mothers in emotional blurbs. Some questions address the basics of how to get through the day, or diaper the baby, or what to feed him and when.

I knew nothing about children. I was an only child and never even baby-sat as a teenager.

— 🍃 —

During pregnancy, I spent a great deal of time preparing for the birth of our child and no time preparing for after the birth. I figured it would come naturally. What a joke!

— 🍃 —

I'm an RN, yet when it comes to my baby and illness, I'm lost. I call the doctor in a panic over every little thing, yet I can give medical advice to my friends about their babies.

As we continue mothering, we move past some of the survival skill questions only to face other questions that focus more on sustenance skills. Fifty-four percent of moms surveyed in a *Redbook* magazine report that they are as good a mother as their own mothers were. However, their confidence declines as their children age and their mothering focus deepens to sustenance issues. Beyond simply surviving, how do we nurture the lives of those who have been entrusted to us?

One thing that surprised me was the realization that I knew so little about raising a child. I'm not talking about what to dress him in or how to feed him but how to cultivate his unique qualities. The awesomeness of this responsibility has only grown larger in the twenty-one months since his birth.

— 🍃 —

I imagined babyhood—then zoomed up to age eight or so when we could take the kids hiking and biking. I forgot about ages one to seven. Help!

— 🍃 —

What do I do when my five-year-old lies (again)? Are my children going to grow up to be productive adults? Are they going to share my belief in God and the values I believe are right? Where does my husband fit in? Am I reading the right books?

The questions are endless:

- How do I get my child to sleep through the night?
- How do my husband and I find time to be alone together?
- How do I get anything done when I have two preschoolers now instead of just one?

- How do I handle my mother-in-law's judgment of how I'm mothering?
- How should I discipline? Should I spank or not? If so, how and until what age? If not, what should I use to discipline?
- When should I try potty-training and how in the world do I do it?
- What about sibling rivalry? The kids are driving me nuts with their fighting!
- How much TV should I let them watch?
- What about schooling? Should we go public, private, or home school?
- Should I stay home with the kids or work outside the home?
- How should I handle money issues?

Whether focused on basic survival skills or on the more complex issues of growth and development, moms of young children are always asking questions. Where will we find the answers we seek?

LIBRARIES OF LEARNING

Five sources provide the bulk of instruction regarding mothering. Most moms find that they need to spend time in all five libraries of learning during their mothering careers.

Maternal Instinct

Every mom has a built-in sense of what her child needs. Pediatrician Dr. William Sears observes, "God would not have given you this child without also giving you the means to care for this child."[1] Even adoptive mothers cite an innate response that seemed to emerge from within them as their new babies were placed in their arms.

Tough to prove and easy to dismiss, the library of maternal instinct is a place where a mom must learn to trust her heart response to her child.

There's a way in which mothering is instinctive. A mom intrinsically knows her child. The library of maternal instinct teaches moms to trust this instinctive response. Few of us have to be taught to cuddle a baby who is upset. Most of us respond immediately to her cry and can quickly interpret its meaning. Sometimes we wake in the night before he even starts to whimper. Having taken no courses on cooing, babbling, or giggling with our infants, we naturally respond when they speak in this "language."

I thought my patience level would be much lower, like when in one week my daughter threw four new rolls of toilet paper, a full bottle of bubble bath, and my car keys in the toilet. Instead of going ballistic, I simply fished the items out and removed my daughter from the bathroom and diverted her attention to something else. I guess I sold myself short on having what it takes to be a good mother. I've also learned that motherhood is twenty-five percent learned knowledge and seventy-five percent instinct.

— ❧ —

There are times I feel uncertain about what to do. But by talking with other parents and listening to my heart, we manage pretty well.

Maternal Knowledge

While some aspects of mothering are instinctive, information about what to do when can be learned. Mothering is a skill that will become easier with knowledge and practice. But some mothers still aren't sure.

When I was pregnant, I took it for granted that mothering would come naturally. The day my baby was born, it hit me like a ton of bricks that mothering did not come naturally to me, and I felt nervous just holding her. I felt totally inadequate as a mother and needed help.

— ❧ —

I graduated from college with honors, but when I had my first baby, I felt so unsure of what to do. I immediately enrolled in parenting classes at the local hospital and read everything I could.

The importance of knowing what to do when must not be minimized. We have to learn what medicines help which illnesses, which foods stop diarrhea, when to expect him to crawl and then walk, and how to child-proof a home.

Herein lies the great balancing act between heart (maternal instinct) and head (maternal knowledge). Maternal instinct may tell you that your child is not feeling very well. Do his eyes look funny? Is he more clingy than normal? Do you sense that something is wrong even though there's no fever? If so, then maternal knowledge will tell you what to do. Take his temperature. Give Tylenol®. Push fluids.

In the library of maternal instinct, we learn to listen to our heart response to our child. In the library of maternal knowledge, we learn to find answers. Maternal instinct is innate. Maternal knowledge is acquired. We must have both, for they function in tandem.

Actions based on instinct alone may lead to overprotection, overreaction, or just plain error. For example, our instinct is to protect our children, but overprotection can paralyze them emotionally. On the other hand, actions based on knowledge alone may overlook subtle truths and harm a sensitive spirit. We need to seek a balance.

Heart Values

Every mom holds to certain core values that she longs to pass on to her children. These values help us make decisions. They inspire us to continue when we'd rather quit. They motivate us to change when we'd rather stay the same. They are our rules for living.

In the library of heart values, we decide intentionally which of these ideals will be communicated and modeled in everyday life—before children, before families, before the world in which we live.

Some of us have operated out of a system of rules that has been in place since we were tiny tots ourselves. Others are building on a small base, enlarging as we grow. And still others are just beginning to come to grips with what really matters and are giving it voice, perhaps for the first time.

What do you want your life to stand for? What passions do you want your children to inherit from you? These principles are your mothering maxims. They are guidelines by which to mother. Truths that direct. Absolutes that we want to see our children adopt as their own. At the end of each chapter, you'll find examples of "mothering maxims."

Need some examples? Here's one: "The goal of mothering is to teach a child not to lean on you. Mothering is to make leaning unnecessary." At the root of this maxim is the belief that a mother's role in the life of her child is to bring up him or her to be an independent individual who can live confidently and competently.

Another? "The Bible is believable today and its principles are applicable to everyday life because the Bible is God's Word." At the core of this maxim is the belief that what the Bible teaches is timelessly true and can be trusted to help us deal with today's challenges. God speaks to us through the Bible.

What are *your* mothering maxims? Knowing what to do in the life of your child, in your marriage, and in your life in general begins with knowing what is really important to you. Before you look outside yourself for help, look *inside* to see what you value and why. (See Building Block #1 at the end of this chapter for help in developing your own mothering maxims.)

Expert Advice

There are answers, answers, and more answers available to the mother with questions. A myriad of sources compose the library of expert advice. At times, the answers bombard us even before we formulate the questions. Most moms spend time wandering through the "rows" of resources available today.

Take the media, for example. In a season when it's very difficult to get out of the house to seek other input, moms of small children are tempted to hold sacred the views of talk shows, soap operas, radio gurus, and women's magazines. While such sources entertain and inform in part, we must ask whether they offer complete and adequate information. Can we trust them?

There is also the medical profession. Many moms rely on helpful advice from their pediatrician or family practitioner. Questions about everything from earaches to diarrhea find solutions on the medical hotline. A must for any mom.

I always thought that motherhood would be easy as long as you went by the book, but it didn't take long for me to realize that there is more than one book, and they all say something different.

I wish I had a single "Answer Book" with all the answers regarding health, disciplining, and development.

And then there are the books. From Dr. Spock to Dr. Terry Brazleton to Dr. James Dobson, volumes of information are available on every subject under the sun.

All this expert advice can be a bit overwhelming.

Moms need some kind of system in order to glean the best from this library of help. Without library tools, we get lost in the card catalog, unsure of where to turn next. Several guidelines might help as we make our way through the maze of expert opinions.

- *Check credentials.* Every expert comes with a background orientation. Before you adopt his or her advice, read the fine print. Where was the author educated? What are her basic assumptions? Do his values agree with your value base, or do they contradict it?
- *Get a second opinion.* Avoid the temptation to become a follower of only one theory. Wisdom often comes from a multiplicity of sources. Gathering more information helps you make good choices.

For instance, when you're selecting a discipline method, research many approaches before you settle on one. And then, throughout your child's development, continue your research and reconsider approaches as her needs change.

- *Be discerning.* Use critical thinking. Ask yourself, Does this approach make sense? Does it contradict my values or common knowledge? Is it consistent with what the Bible teaches?
- *Put advice to a test.* Once you discover some advice you think might work, try it out. If it doesn't, adapt it to suit your child's needs. If it still doesn't work, throw it out and go on to another idea.

One principle from a marriage expert may be appropriate, whereas another may not fit at all. For example, a suggested method of time management may be helpful in the early years of mothering, for instance, and then become useless as your children age. Before integrating advice into your life and the life of your family, try it out.

The library of expert opinion is one of the most well-stocked sources of instruction available to the mother of preschoolers. But before you start picking resources off the shelf at random, learn how to use this library. Devise a system of discernment that works for you.

Mothering Mentors

In *Virtue* magazine, Beth Sharpton speaks of the heart-desire of many moms: "Most of my knowledge about woman-liness and mothering has come from books, but I long for a friend who has persevered through childrearing and other stages of life who will teach me through her example and experience."[2]

The library of mentorship can offer moms instruction on how to manage time, relationships, and mothering from an up-close-and-personal perspective. Traditionally, a woman's mother assumed this role and instructed her daughter in how to care for an infant and other family-related issues. Unfortunately, many women today don't live near their mothers or have that kind of relationship with their mothers, so the role of mentoring is assumed by others.

In the Greek legend, *The Odyssey,* Mentor was the faithful friend to Ulysses. When Ulysses went to fight in the Trojan War, the care and education of his son, Telemachus, was entrusted to Mentor. In time, the term *mentor* has become a synonym for a wise person, a trusted advisor, a counselor, or teacher.

A mothering mentor is a woman who has scaled the mountain you intend to climb. She's gone before you. She knows the path. She knows the toeholds. She comes alongside you and offers encouragement that you, too, can make it. From her own life experience, she can teach on such subjects as how to mother, how to organize life, how to develop your abilities and character. For a young mother who has never seen good mothering in practice before, she might model mothering. She might give a glimpse of what marriage looks like down the road or how to hurdle difficult spots in friendship.

A mothering mentor is not a know-it-all. She's not an expert with degrees and credentials trailing after her name, although she might possess formal training. She's simply a mom who's made it through some of the most challenging years of mothering. She's learned from her mistakes, enjoyed a few successes, and can now share her insights with those of us who are coming along behind.

In the local MOPS group, mentors are modeled in the "Titus woman" principle, found in Titus 2:3–4: "Teach the older women to be reverent in the way they live . . . to teach what is good. Then they can train the younger women to love their husbands and children, to be self-controlled and pure, to be busy at home, to be kind, and to be subject to their husbands, so that no one will malign the word of God." Ideally, each group benefits from a mentoring mom who shares gently and practically from her life experiences in a group setting and is then available for one-on-one advice.

Mentors are all around us. They are found in churches, in families, in cross-generational friendships. If you're eager to find a mentoring mother, look for qualities like honesty, wisdom, discernment, and encouragement. Watch from a distance before pursuing a relationship. Then, work up your courage and ask if you can poke around a bit to see how she does what she does with her kids. Mentoring doesn't have to be a formal arrangement, nor will you always learn everything you need to know from one single person.

Peers

Probably the most common source for moms comes through relationships with other moms.

A woman asks a co-worker over the next cubicle what she should do with her unruly toddler. Neighbors swap theories while their preschoolers race around on their tricycles. Though many mothers are separated physically or emotionally from the extended families that could help, some live close enough to relatives to rely on their input.

As a mother of small children, I need to talk to other moms who share my concerns and take an active part in the mental, emotional, and especially the spiritual development of their children.

Many moms are involved in churches where support and instruction come hand in hand. Mother's Day Out programs, support groups, or cross-generational relationships offer instruction needed in topics ranging from discipline to budgeting.

Whether formal or spontaneous, in groups or one-on-one, moms need the supportive community of their peers. After being up all night with a crying baby, a mom finds comfort in chatting on the phone with a friend who also got no sleep. Ah, the support! The camaraderie! The comfort! The answers!

Check out a church nearby for a MOPS group. There you'll find

I recently was struggling with the amount of time my children were spending watching television. I recalled another mom who had once described her solution to this problem—issuing tickets to watch each TV program. I called her and we shared for over an hour on the phone. Within three weeks, my children were "weaned" to a minimal amount of TV every day!

— 🍂 —

I heard a speaker on sibling rivalry and then gleaned hints from discussing what was said with others who attended. My kids still fight, but I'm armed with some sound new ideas to help along the way!

a ready-made audience of women with similar interests. Head to the park on a sunny day and you'll probably locate other moms with kids the ages of your kids. The library of peers offers the kind of practical advice moms need.

A MOTHER'S MISSION

While children come into the world without an instruction manual, many libraries of learning are available to the mom of young children. Susan Lenzkes' simple poem illustrates our desire to mother the right way while directing us to relax in a trusting posture:

> I searched—
> but there definitely was not
> a packet of instructions
> attached to my children
> when they arrived.
> And none has since
> landed in my mailbox.
> Lord, show me how
> to be a good parent.
> Teach me to
> correct without crushing,
> help without hanging on,
> listen without laughing,
> surround without smothering,
> and love without limit—
> the way You love me.[3]

Used by permission,
copyright Susan L. Lenzkes, 1981.
Available through author.

BUILDING BLOCKS

BUILDING BLOCK #1:

Develop your own Mothering Maxims.

Maxims are the memorable sayings or statements that shape your attitudes and actions. They sum up your values. Write some of your own. Here are some questions to get you started, from Cindy Tolliver's book *At-Home Motherhood:*

- Think back to your own childhood. What things did your own mother do that really made a difference in your life? List at least three.
- What things did your mother do that you would like to do differently? List at least three.
- Think about notable mothers you know. What do these women do that you might want to make one of your own missions? Write down three.
- List at least ten goals of mothering. Here are a few guidelines:
    - Let your ideas flow. This is brainstorming, not English 101. There are no right answers.
    - Make your statements "I-oriented" and active. In other words, don't make your mission dependent on others doing something for you.
    - Make your statements concrete. Instead of saying, "I want to start having fun with my kids," say, "I want to plan at least one fun activity a week with the kids."
    - Pick the five that are the most important to you. This doesn't mean you aren't going to accomplish the others, but if you have too many goals, your attention will be spread too thin.[4]

BUILDING BLOCK #2:

Discover your learning style.

When it comes to instruction, everyone has a unique style by which they learn best. Here are some questions to help determine your own unique style. Read the question or statement, then circle your most appropriate answer. Some will be difficult, but try to respond in the way you might react the majority of the time.

1. You will usually remember more from a class lecture when:
   a. you do not take notes but listen very closely.
   b. you sit near the front of the room and watch the speaker.
   c. you take notes (whether or not you look at them again).

2. You usually solve problems by:
   a. talking to yourself or a friend.
   b. using an organized, systematic approach with lists, schedules, etc.
   c. walking, pacing, or other physical activities.

3. You remember phone numbers when you can't write them down by:
   a. repeating it orally to yourself.
   b. "seeing" or "visualizing" the number in your mind.
   c. sketching out the numbers with your finger on a table or wall.

4. You have to learn something new and it would be easier if you could:
   a. be told how to do it.
   b. watch a demonstration of how to do it.
   c. try it yourself.

5. You remember most from a movie by:
   a. what the characters said, the background noises and music.
   b. the setting, scenery, and costumes or uniforms.
   c. the feelings you had.

6. You go to the grocery store and you:
   a. silently or orally repeat the list to yourself.
   b. walk up and down the aisles to see what you need.
   c. usually remember what you need from your forgotten list at home.

7. You are trying to remember something so you:
   a. hear what was said or noises that happened in your head.
   b. try to see it happen in your mind.
   c. feel the way it reacted with your emotions.

8. You learn a foreign language best by:
   a. listening to record or tapes.
   b. using workbooks and writing.
   c. attending a typical class where you read and write.

9. You are confused on the spelling of a word so you:
   a. sound it out.
   b. try to see it written in your mind.
   c. try writing it several different ways and choosing the one that looks right.

10. You enjoy reading most when you can read:
    a. dialogue between characters.
    b. passages that use mostly description that allows you to create mental pictures.
    c. stories with a lot of action early in the book; you have a hard time sitting still.

11. You usually remember people you have met by their:
    a. names (you forget faces).
    b. faces (you forget names).
    c. walk, mannerisms, motions.

12. You are mostly distracted by:
   a. noises.
   b. people.
   c. environment (temperature, comfort of furniture, etc.).

13. You usually dress:
   a. fairly well but clothes are not so important to you.
   b. in a particular style and neatly.
   c. comfortably so you can move around.

14. You can't do anything physical or read, so you could choose to:
   a. talk with a friend.
   b. watch TV or look through a window.
   c. move slightly in your chair or bed.

Scoring:

Count the total number of responses for each letter and write them in the blanks below:

   a. Auditory (learn best by hearing) _____
   b. Visual (learn best by seeing) _____
   c. Kinesthetic (learn best by touching, doing, moving)[5]

   _____

BUILDING BLOCK #3:

Develop critical thinking skills.

Mothers make decisions every day. Here are some suggestions for evaluating choices and making wise decisions.

1. *Pinpoint the problem.* State specifically what it is you need to decide.
2. *Set a deadline.* Give yourself a "due date" for your decision. Develop a time line.
3. *Gather information.* What are your sources? Where can you get the facts?

4. *List the pros and cons.* What are the positive and negative aspects of each alternative?
5. *Ask tough questions.* Evaluate your options according to your values. Does this fit? Is it wise? Does it conflict with biblical truth?
6. *Make a decision.* Move forward in a direction with confidence that you've done the best job you can.

BUILDING BLOCK #4:

Find a mentor.

- Determine your mentoring needs. Do you need a coach, an encourager, a counselor, or someone to listen to your ideas? Do you want to sharpen your leadership or parenting skills, gifts, or spiritual depth? Your needs and goals will determine what kind of mentor is best. You don't need a mentor unless you have goals.
- Who are the resourceful people you already know and respect? An aunt or close relative? A godly woman? An older neighbor or friend? Relationships and resourcefulness act as magnets and serve as the basis of the mentoring relationship. Look for women six to fifteen years older than you are. Too much older, and she will be part of an unfamiliar generation. Too much younger and she will be too much like a peer. Sometimes you can be mentored by a woman younger than yourself if she has unusual qualities or expertise.
- Look for women who are living your dream or share in your dream. Share your desires and objectives with potential mentors. Many older women will be flattered that you consider them worthy of your consideration. Remember, they have a need for generativity—impacting the succeeding generation.
- Be willing to pay the price to be mentored. This includes flexibility and commitment. If she jogs, jog with her.

Offer to work on a project together so you can help her as you learn from her. Approach your time together with specific needs and questions. A resourceful person will be able to give you great input without formal preparation. Your initiative and intentionality will speed and enhance the mentoring process.[6]

BUILDING BLOCK #5:

Build up your resources.

1. Begin to accumulate a few books and tapes. Start with some suggestions from the lists "For Further Reading" at the end of each chapter. Visit your local Christian bookstore or contact Focus on the Family at the following numbers: To request books or tapes, call 1-800-A-FAMILY. For additional information, please call (719) 531-5181.
2. Take a personal field trip to your local library. Don't be intimidated by the computerized listing of books. Someone is always happy to help you. Take advantage of this valuable resource.
3. Establish a lending library with your friends. Trade tapes, books, and magazines.
4. Get a subscription to *Christian Parenting Today*. (For information, call 1-800-238-2221.)

FOR FURTHER READING:

Born to Fly: How to Discover and Encourage Your Child's Natural Gifts (and Workbook), Thom Black

Christian Parenting and Child Care, William Sears, M.D.

How to Single Parent, Dr. Fitzhugh Dobson

Managing Your Money, Ron Blue

Once a Month Cooking, Mimi Wilson and Mary Beth Lagerborg

Traits of a Healthy Family, Delores Curran
Using Your Money Wisely, Larry Burkett
The Way They Learn, Cynthia Ulrich Tobias
What to Expect When You're Expecting, and *What to Expect the First Year,* Arlene Eisenberg, Heidi E. Murkoff, Hathaway, BSN

Mothering Maxim

— ❧ —

An informed mother
knows best.

Six

Help:

Sometimes I need to share the load

What time are the Jacksons coming over tonight?" Randy called to Susan from his comfy chair in front of the TV, the remote control poised in his hand.

Randy had just gotten home from work and looked beat. Besides, Susan knew her husband liked to relax on Friday nights. "Six o'clock," she called back as she rushed to put some bowls in the dishwasher. "In about ten minutes."

She looked forward to having the Jacksons over. Their kids were about the same ages and played well together, which gave the adults a chance to talk without the normal interruptions.

Susan quickly took stock of her dinner preparations. The table was set and the meal basically ready, but Legos® still littered the family room floor. And a few stray Playdoh® crumbs crunched under her feet as she shoved the casserole in the oven. Just then the children ran screeching from the bathroom to their bedrooms down the hall.

The bathroom. Ugh! She hadn't cleaned the bathroom yet. She peered across the room at Randy, who was still changing channels. Throwing the hot pads on the counter, she took long strides down the hall to the bathroom and flipped on the light. What a mess. Toilet paper hung from everywhere two feet high and under. Meagan and Steven couldn't reach above that. The rest of the roll of paper floated in the toilet. She heard giggles from behind the closed bedroom door down the hall.

Then the doorbell rang.

"Su-u-uszzz! They're here!" Randy yelled.

Stifling a scream, Susan fished the wet roll of paper out and threw it in the wastebasket. She reached for the only towel that matched the bathroom, but it was missing. Then she spotted it—a wet wad stuck behind the toilet.

The doorbell rang again. The kids burst from their rooms and ran down the hall toward the front door, giggling and banging against the walls.

"Su-u-uszzz! They're here! Aren't you going to get the door?" Randy called again.

A high-pitched wail emerged from the bathroom. Forming words, the voice screeched, "Hey—am I the *only* one who can answer the door? Am I the *only* one who can make dinner and clean up and watch the kids?" As Susan scooped up the towel from behind the toilet, she realized that the voice was hers. "HEY—DOES ANYONE OUT THERE REALIZE I COULD USE SOME HELP?! I SAID, HELP!!!!!"

THE TOUGHEST QUESTION

When mothers of preschoolers were asked, "What do you need most?" they offered a smattering of answers. Here are some:

> *A housekeeper*
> *A nanny*
> *A secretary*
> *Another set of arms*
> *To get organized*
> *Help*

Other moms described the difference between expectations and reality:

> *I find myself screaming and getting frustrated and I know that's not what I'm supposed to be doing. Sometimes I feel like I'm losing my mind. I need help!*

— ❧ —

> *I always thought the father would help out a lot more.*

While we might blurt out confessions like these, when it comes down to everyday life, most of us have a difficult time actually asking for help. Griping comes more easily. We whine and even scream on occasion. And many of us have mastered the martyr role, in which we carry on our work while sighing frequently and loudly, in hopes that someone will notice our weariness and step in to help. But when it comes to asking for specific assistance, our lips button shut in discomfort.

Why? Because some of us feel that asking for help is a sign of weakness, and we don't want to appear weak. As mothers, our jobs are to handle whatever comes with patience and immediate solutions. When a broken toy is tearfully brought to us, we superglue it back together. When an outfit is soiled, we wash it. When the refrigerator is empty, we fill it. When the milk spills, we clean it up. It doesn't occur to some of us to enlist help until we're tied up in knots of legitimate commitments or are completely out of gas, frustrated, and broken down with fatigue.

Further, we feel guilty about asking for help. Just admitting that we can't DO IT ALL and could use some help feels like admitting failure. Use a playpen? How could we?! Let the baby cry? No way! Make a microwave dinner? Are you kidding?! Mothers of preschoolers don't have occasional guilt. We have "perma-guilt," ever-present in the wear of life. If we don't "make it from scratch" every time, it doesn't count.

As much as we'd like to have some help and desperately need help, we refrain from actually asking for it. For some reason, the toughest question we may ever have to ask is "Will you help me?"

HELP YOURSELF

Learning to help yourself is the first step in conquering this need for help. Maybe you're a single mom and it's all you can do just to get the kids to day care, handle the day's work, and then get them back home and fed again in the evening. Or maybe you're married but your husband works long hours, or travels all week, or works nights, or simply isn't interested in his family role. "Help? Ha! Where can I go to find help?" you ask.

Partners in Parenting

Moms of young children need help from a myriad of sources. The Bible encourages us to turn to others: "Two are better than one, because they have a good return for their work: If one falls down, his friend can help him up. But pity the man who falls and has no one to help him up!" (Eccl. 4:9–10).

Who are your partners in parenting? Your best friend? Your husband? Your doctor? Your child's preschool teacher? A home schooling networking group? A baby-sitter? Your next-door neighbor? A grandmother? From extended family to the friends who have become your chosen family, to community and church resources, you have partners in parenting. Though a mother is always "on duty," she can partner with others to share the responsibility. An old African proverb states that it takes a whole village to bring up a child.

Helping yourself first means recognizing the importance of partnering in parenting.

Ask for help.

Help is available. But we have to learn to help ourselves.

We have to recognize and admit that sometimes we can't do it all. We don't have to feel guilty about appearing weak and admitting this normal need. But we do have to learn to ask. Directly, by using words. No one can read your mind. No one is going to waltz in, recognize your predicament, and save you.

I needed to go to the dentist. My mother couldn't take care of the kids. I was used to handling things on my own and didn't want to ask my friend. But I had to ... and she didn't mind at all.

Remember that you weren't meant to be all things at all times to your children. That's not healthy for them or for us. Relinquish some control over some areas of responsibility. Share the load as well as the laurels. You may discover that you are not as indispensable as you thought, but you'll be more sane.

If you want help, if you truly want to share the load, ask for the help you need.

FRIENDS AS HELPERS

A natural place to ask for help is to ask a friend. Mom and author Donna Partow confesses this slow but sure discovery in her book, *No More Lone Ranger Moms*: "This motherhood trip wasn't designed for lone rangers. It takes more than one woman against the world to raise a child in this increasingly complex and dangerous world. Even the pioneers sometimes circled the wagons. Women need one another. It's time to circle the wagons."[1]

When my toddler fell on the fireplace hearth, I panicked! My husband was at work and we were new in the neighborhood. What else could I do? I grabbed a towel and my child and ran next door. Thank goodness, my neighbor was home! She bundled up her little one and raced me to the emergency room.

One-on-One Help

When you finally get up the nerve to ask a friend for help, you may be pleasantly surprised by the response.

The result of receiving help one-on-one outweighs the risk of asking. In fact, many long-lasting friendships between women begin this way.

Bartering: Trading Tasks

Bartering is an old-fashioned term to describe task-trading. Ideally, moms come together and meet their individual needs by swapping strengths. Bartering is a way to receive the help you need without spending the money you don't have. Bartering also makes it possible to spend more time on tasks you enjoy doing while allowing someone else to fill in on duties you don't enjoy as much. If you are a wallpaper whiz but hate to garden, swap talents with a neighbor. If you love to cook, but not with kids in the kitchen, arrange for your friend to watch all the kids while you cook for both families.

Support Groups

Support groups are not for the addicted or the bankrupt only. Support groups are for all sorts of people who come together to meet common needs. Mothers of young children especially benefit by forming or joining support groups.

> *I first came to MOPS (Mothers of Preschoolers) when a friend invited me. As I sat there with that group of women, I thought to myself,* How pathetic. I'm at a support group. Have I really sunk this low? *After I went through a complete session, I realized it was much more. It was fun and exciting to learn in all different areas and to help solve problems by sharing with other women.*

Set up a baby-sitting co-op. Consider a food co-op to get discount prices on large quantities. Join a support group on parenting issues where you can gather with others struggling with the same questions and concerns.

Friends are a readily available source of help. They offer comfort, a sense of community, and practical assistance.

HUSBAND HELP

If you're married, the most obvious source of help is your husband. But expecting help from him may not always be feasible.

> *I'm married but sometimes feel like a single mom because my husband works twelve to fourteen hours a day, six days a week.*

Or maybe he's not aware that you could use some help.

> *My kids place their food and drink orders all day. My husband stays after work to have a beer, comes home, eats, and goes to bed. I feel like no one thought of me at all the whole day.*

Or maybe he doesn't understand the kind of help you need.

When the kids whine and cry, my husband tells me not to let them get to me. He tells me what to do, instead of helping with them.

Or maybe you feel he works so hard that you shouldn't ask for his help at home. And when you do ask, you feel guilty.

Sometimes I feel myself hitting my limit and know I need some help. I realize I need to ask for help and not feel bad about it but I find it difficult to ask, especially when my husband has had a long week at work.

— ❧ —

I feel so guilty asking for help. He has a full-time job, and mothering is my full-time job.

What about the issue of roles? What is the mom's job and what is the dad's? How do we sort through who does what?

My husband comes home and my son wants Daddy. They play and have fun, and I feel invisible. I feel like I work all the time—if not with my son then in the house. When my husband comes home from work, his job is done and playtime starts.

Sometimes, when you ask for help, you get no response. So rather than raise an issue, you do it yourself.

One Saturday I was supposed to watch both kids, clean and vacuum, do the dishes and laundry, get dinner, and still have time to relax with my husband. It didn't work because he wouldn't help out. So I ended up doing everything myself.

Is it realistic to expect a husband to help? And if so, how do we translate these expectations into reality?

Clarify a co-parenting partnership.

In order to mother most effectively, we're wise to define what we expect the contribution of mothers and fathers to be in parenting. Are both parents? Are both responsible for the development and health of a child?

In her book, *Becoming a Woman of Strength,* Ruth Barton writes:

The most encouraging thing that has happened for me as a mother is that Chris (my husband) and I have begun seeing ourselves more clearly as a team in this challenge-of-a-lifetime called parenting. I have found that I do not need another book on how to be a better mother. . . . What I have needed is my husband, the father of these children, to participate more fully with me in this great call of God upon our lives. I have needed to hear him say with words and with action, "You are not alone. These children are just as much my responsibility as they are yours."

God's instruction for us to attend to our children is huge and multifaceted, but when men and women are committed to it together, it is much less overwhelming.[2]

Research shows that mothers and fathers parent in different ways and are able to provide for unique needs in their children. Whereas the mother is the primary source of attachment, so necessary for infant bonding and future social relationships, the father is the main source for increasing the child's physical and intellectual independence. Infants value their fathers' "optimally novel stimuli." They are not so unfamiliar as to provoke stranger anxiety, but they come and go often enough to stimulate interest as "exciting novelties."[3]

Developing a co-parenting style takes work and patience. It requires honest self-examination and careful communication.

Take a long, hard look at your parenting style. If you're running the family ship like the captain of the fleet, issuing orders and demanding compliance, you may be able to enjoy a sense of control, but you won't see help coming forth from your husband. A willingness to help comes from a shared sense of ownership of responsibility. Are your children *your* children or are they your husband's children as well?

Carefully observe your behavior for a few

There are so many demands on our time that it feels like tag-team parenting. I watch our son while my husband works. My husband watches him while I fix dinner. I watch him while my husband mows the lawn. Now we're trying to make an effort to do this together.

days. Do you leave detailed lists about how to diaper, feed, and play with the baby when you are away, or do you allow your husband the freedom to figure out what works for him? When he's on duty for a morning or an evening with the children, do you label the activity *baby-sitting* or is it *parenting*? *Baby-sitting* implies he is temporarily taking over your responsibility, while *parenting* denotes shared responsibilities. Even subtle words like these can communicate that what he is doing as a father is as meaningful as what you do as a mother.

If we want help, we must examine our behavior and be willing to make adjustments in order to create the potential for the co-parenting partnership.

Ask your husband for help.

It takes many people to bring up a child. A mother can't do it all by herself. No one can. If your sources of help include a husband, clarify your co-parenting responsibilities, then ask him for help!

Here's how:

• *Ask clearly and directly.* Don't hint. Don't sigh or pout. Don't expect him to read your mind or even notice your needs. Tell him. Put your request in words.

> "I need help with the housework. Would you please vacuum for me?"
>
> "I need to go to the shopping mall without having to worry about Rachel running around. Would you please watch her tonight while I go?"
>
> "I need help with the grocery shopping this week. Would you be willing to go this time?"

If this is the first time you've asked your husband for help, choose a calm moment to do so. Resist the urge to strike out angrily in a moment of frustration or panic with accusations: "You *never* help!" Instead, at the beginning of a day that you know will be stressful, sit down and state your need clearly and without a lot of explanation, justification, or emotion.

• *Live with the results.* If you ask your husband to vacuum, resist the urge to critique his work. If you ask him to take Rachel while you shop, then embrace his choices as to what he does with her while you're away. If you send him to the grocery store, enjoy his purchases when he returns.

The fact is clear. If you want help, receive it in the form in which it comes. He may not do it exactly as you would, but criticizing his help may cause him to withdraw it altogether.

• *Risk.* It may appear risky to change a pattern of relating or communicating in a marriage. If your husband has grown accustomed to your being a "Supermom/Superwoman," he may have a hard time readjusting to your new requests or admission that you need help. Give him time. Gently reassure him that you're not abdicating your nurturing role in the family but that you are just recognizing your needs and limits and facing the fact that you can't do it all.

Undoubtedly, there will be times when your husband will simply refuse your requests. Learn to respond without an outburst of emotion. Receive his no the way you would want him to receive *your* no. But don't stop asking. Find another opportunity when you need his help and ask again.

Ask clearly. Live with the results. Be willing to risk. But understand that husband help grows out of a growing relationship. When you invest yourself in a loving relationship with your husband, you can learn to ask for the help you need and he can learn to offer it.

MOTHER'S LITTLE HELPERS

How do you get your children to help?

Some scoff at the mere thought. "I'd rather do it myself," most of us say, after nagging them unsuccessfully or refusing to live with the quality of results.

Others make a joke of the idea of motivating children to help out. It has been said that there are three ways to get something done: Do it yourself, hire someone, or forbid your kids to do it.

But there is another tactic. You can *train* your children to help. Through a deliberate choice of the will, careful follow-through, and much determination, you can turn your children into mother's little helpers.

Why Training Our Children to Help Is Good

There are two reasons why training our children to help us is a good idea:

- Learning to help mom is good for children.
  In her book *Do I Have To?* Patricia Sprinkle suggests that the "ultimate purpose of parenting is to help our children move out of our lives."[4] If she's right, then we'd better start empowering our preschool-aged children to begin to do for themselves now what they will need to do for themselves later.
  Cooking, cleaning, and laundering are skills that must be taught by instruction and repetition. A child does not automatically begin to exercise these skills when he or she turns eighteen, without instruction. Further, the skills learned in one's nuclear family will be reflected in their future families and working relationships. What we teach our children now will make a difference in who they become later.
- Learning to help mom is good for mom.
  Ah, to come home and find the dinner table already set! Or to see a toddler struggling to make a bed and then triumphing in the result! To climb into a bathtub that was cleaned after the last use! Or to return to a kitchen where cereal bowls have been stacked in the sink or put in the dishwasher instead of being left on the table, surrounded by puddles of milk! Such help is good for mom!

How to Help Your Children Help

Obviously, we can't expect much in the way of help from children under the age of two. But even toddlers can begin to "help Mommy" with small tasks.

- *Select age-appropriate tasks for your children.* Ask the younger ones to put away plastic containers, pick up their toys, or put their dirty clothes in the hamper. In this stage of developing independence, such chores can actually assist their feeling of doing things "all by myself." Increasing responsibilities as the age of your children increases will keep them motivated and challenged.

- *Motivate your children with rewards.* Whether it's verbal praise, an allowance, a treat, or something else you deem appropriate, motivate your children to be helpers. Be sure to withhold rewards until tasks are complete because we also are teaching them about logical consequences. But once the tasks are satisfactorily completed, give the rewards with gusto!

- *Adjust your standards of a job well-done.* Children will often mess up more than they clean up as they begin the helping process. Steel yourself during these days. Your response to initial efforts will set the tone for future attempts. If a child feels unsuccessful, he or she may not want to risk further failure. Reward the effort and the attitude more than the perfection of the task completed.

With patience and persistence, mother's little helpers can grow into mom's main helpers.

HELPING YOUR HELPERS

Whether you find help in your husband, a child, a day care center, a school, or a church, learn to maximize your help by helping your helpers.

Learn the art of delegation. Delegation actually makes it possible to multiply your presence and your impact and your time while developing others' skills.

In her book, *Thriving as a Working Woman,* Gwen Ellis applies delegation principles from the working world to home life. She offers action points that can be adapted for the mother of preschoolers.

1. Decide what you want done. Set goals and make them measurable and specific.
2. If your needs or circumstances change, inform your helpers. For example, your baby-sitter needs to know if you're beginning to potty-train your toddler, along with some guidelines about the way you are approaching this challenge.
3. Pick the right person for the job.
4. Train the person for the job.
5. Check on your helper without hovering.
6. Be available for further training.
7. Give your helper the whole task. Resist the urge to go back in there and finish up once you've assigned a task.
8. Try not to give the same "awful" job to the same person time after time. Rotate the more disliked tasks among family members.
9. Keep cool when someone makes a mistake.[5]

If we want our helpers to be all the help they can be, we need to help them help.

EMOTIONAL HELP

Sometimes when moms cry out for help, the need is not physical but emotional, and sometimes that need can't be met by those around us. Sometimes you will feel helplessly overwhelmed and wonder if you need professional help. How do you know?

First, be careful not to mistake a need for help as necessarily a need for professional help. "There's a great temptation to look at other people and think: 'She's got two children and she can really handle it,'" Susan Yates admits. "'I'm about to die with one! What's wrong with me?' We are all made differently and we have different levels of cope-ability."[6]

How do you know if you've reached your limit of cope-ability? Most professionals agree that there are certain symptoms of psychological ill health:

- If you are in danger of hurting yourself or your children either verbally or physically, you need professional help.
- If you exhibit the symptoms of depression: loss of or increase in appetite, apathy, increased or decreased sleep, you may need professional help.
- If you think you are addicted to a drug or alcohol, you probably need professional help.

Areas of professional input can include self-development, marriage, sexual issues, childrearing issues, and physical issues.

To find a professional who can be of help, contact your local church, your insurance company, or your medical doctor. Friends are also a good source of referrals when your comfort level allows you to ask.

THE ULTIMATE HELPER

Lastly, we should recognize that there is a greater and free source of help that's available to every mother of preschoolers, merely for the asking. The psalmist tells us that "God is our refuge and strength, an ever-present help in trouble" (Ps. 46:1). God is always present, ready to offer us the most consistent help we could find. When we turn to him in prayer, he hears and responds with love and care.

Help is there for you, Mom. But getting help begins by helping yourself to identify its sources and then learning to ask for it. That may feel uncomfortable at first, but the risk is worth the reward. Take the first step toward that goal today. ❧

BUILDING BLOCKS

M **BUILDING BLOCK #1:**

Work at networking.

Networking is a concept borrowed from the business world that also works in a mother's world, especially in the midst of organized support systems, such as MOPS. In her book *No More Lone Ranger Moms,* Donna Partow offers this advice about networking in groups, which she describes as hard work:

> That's why meeting new people is called Net*working* not net-*sitting* or net-*eating*. It's hard work to reach out and ask for the support you need. It's harder still to *offer help.*

> Instead of sitting back and soaking in, get actively involved. Offer to bring refreshments or to help out by teaching a craft. Invite some of the women to your home during the week, or perhaps invite several women and their husbands over for a Saturday afternoon barbecue. Chances are, the other mothers in the group struggle with the exact same issues you face. Don't wait for someone to reach out to you, take the initiative and set the pace.[7]

O **BUILDING BLOCK #2:**

Find quality child care.

At some point all moms with preschoolers come face to face with the need to find quality child care. Whether it's sporadic or ongoing regular care you seek, the same principles apply. Look for:

- *A shared set of common values.* Will your child-care provider support the values you want to instill in your child? Do you hold the same view of TV-watching? Will the discipline be consistent with what you do at home?

Asking pointed questions of potential care-givers and their references will help you determine who will most consistently follow the beliefs and standards you hold dear.

- *Flexibility.* Look for someone who is willing to accommodate your needs and schedule and work with your child, taking into account your child's individual bent or personality. Honestly communicate your needs and expectations, then listen carefully to their responses.

- *Communication skills.* Knowing what's happening with your child is important. Look for someone willing to share openly what happened when your child was away from you. What did your child do? Were there any unusual behaviors? Did something special happen? Ask questions and expect answers!

- *Commitment to safety.* Knowing that your precious child is in safe hands gives you peace of mind and lets you enjoy your time away. Child care providers should take your child's safety seriously. Look for possible safety hazards. Is the primary focus your child or are the providers easily distracted? What do they consider to be age-appropriate activities for your child? Accidents can and do happen, but look for a conscientious attitude.

- *Consistency.* Look for someone you can count on regularly, rather than a myriad of different baby-sitters. Familiarity builds trust and security in children.

The options are varied: at-home care or away; teenage sitters, college students, or older adults; baby-sitting co-ops where moms trade hours or Mom's Day Out preschool programs. For recommendations, ask family members, or close friends and neighbors. Check with a church, your own or another local one. Get the opinions of other parents. Visit and ask questions. Always consider what is best for your child. Take your time, be observant, and trust your own instincts, your child's responses, and God's guidance.

BUILDING BLOCK #3:

Train mother's little helpers.

Invest in your most obvious and constant helpers with these suggestions for preschoolers. Patricia Sprinkle lists these age-appropriate tasks in her book, *Do I Have To?*:

Tasks for Two- and Three-Year-Olds

load spoons into dishwasher	dust furniture
help feed animals	dig and pull weeds in garden
put away toys after play	fold dishtowels
wipe table	put away silverware
dry unbreakable dishes	load washer, unload dryer
sweep (small broom)	wipe mirrors (parent sprays)
stir orange juice	assist with stirring in cooking
entertain infant	brush teeth, wash face
bring in newspaper	tidy magazines, sofa pillows
mop small area	pick up trash in yard
pour milk (small pitcher)	set table (from diagram)
empty wastebaskets	dress and undress

Additional Tasks for Four- and Five-Year-Olds

put away own clothes	hang towels after bath
clean mirrors and glass alone	plant seeds
set a complete table	grate cheese
clean bathroom sinks	carry own dishes to sink
help with simple desserts	mix salads
help load dishwasher	put away groceries
take dirty clothes to hamper	sort wash loads by color
sort clean laundry	bring in the mail and put in proper place[8]

Cleaning Games for Preschoolers

1. *Colors and Shapes:* Say to your child, "Let's pick up all the red toys. Now let's pick up all the blue ones." "Let's pick up all the squares and rectangles. Now the toys with round parts." "Let's put all the glasses into the dishwasher. Now let's put in all the plates."

2. *Observer Game:* Say, "You put away ten things and let's see if I can remember them in order. Mary, put away a ball. Mary, put away a ball and a truck. Mary, put away a ball, a truck, and a doll."

3. *Dust Muppet or Monster:* Draw a face on a large white sock for a dust mitt that "eats" dust.

4. *Family Army Game:* Put on march music. Line up at attention, then march around the room picking up toys and putting them away in time to the music. When done, report back to the "General" (parent or older child) and salute.

5. *Ant Legion:* Read Proverbs 6:6 and talk about how hard ants work, then pronounce everyone an ant. The ants work hard and fast to see how quickly they can clean a room.

6. *Do It With Me:* Say, "You make one side of the bed and I'll make the other." "You vacuum the room while I dust it." "You clean the mirror while I clean the lavatory." Tell jokes while you work together.

7. *Surprise Me!* Parent leaves the room after asking the child to see how much can get done before the parent returns. Pops right back in and says, "I was just teasing this time, but you don't know when I'll be back next time, do you?" Return when you think the job may be done.

8. *"This Is the Way We . . .":* Remember that old song? Sing together as you do the chore. How many times do you have to sing it before the job is done?

9. *Go Shopping:* Fill a wagon, buggy, or box with toys to be put away, pretending you are shopping, "Oh, I think I'll buy this bear. What will you buy?"

10. *Beat the Clock:* Agree to work ten minutes. Set a timer.[9]

How to Teach a Child a Skill

1. Be familiar with the skill you are going to teach.
2. Develop a logical way to present it.

3. Take the children with you to get materials so they will be able to find them alone later.
4. Name what you are going to teach.
5. Give the children your full attention.
6. Present the lesson carefully and precisely.
7. Use no more language than is necessary.
8. In general, move from left to right.
9. Let the children join in the tasks as soon as they are ready.
10. If children make a mistake, don't draw attention to it.
11. Stay with the children until you are sure they can work alone.
12. Allow the children to work as long as they wish at this new skill.[10]

BUILDING BLOCK #4:

Tips for Single Moms

Single moms face some issues and challenges that are different from those of two-parent families. Such issues include dealing with finances and facing a greater need for partners in parenting.

For financial advice contact Christian Financial Concepts (for books, tapes, and booklets) headed by Larry Burkett, P.O. Box 2377, Gainesville, GA 30503, 1-800-722-1976.

To find other partners in parenting, here are some suggestions:

• Become involved in a church that understands and ministers to single parents—one that includes singles in their family activities and sponsors care groups that involve people in all situations. Although a singles group is good for some of your social needs, you also need to develop relationships with couples in the church.

• Look to the church and your family for healthy male role models for your children. Take the time to pray and watch. Observe some of the fathers in your church to see who handles discipline and fun well. Choose someone who honors his wife and his children. Ask the wife to ask the husband if it would be all right to take one or more of your children along on some family functions. Maybe the family would include your children on a fishing or ski trip. Explain your children's need to experience a healthy Christian family with a strong, male role model.

- It is important for you to get as much help as you can in raising your children. Make sure you have a woman mentor. As a single mom, you have a pressing need to be able to discuss parenting issues with someone. Who better than someone who has been there before and can share her experience with you? Work with a mentor who is sensitive and has been successful as a mother—someone you can confide in. If possible, look to someone who has had more than one child and understands different temperaments and discipline issues.[11]

For further resources:

- Parents Without Partners, 8807 Colesville Rd., Silver Spring, MD 20910, (301) 588-9354. This is the largest organization devoted to the welfare and interests of single parents and their children. The group publishes *The Single Parent* magazine and other resource materials.
- Big Brothers and Sisters of America, 230 North 13th St., Philadelphia, PA 19107, (215) 567-2748. The national headquarters maintains lists of local agencies working with children from single-parent homes.
- Focus on the Family, Colorado Springs, CO 90993, (719) 531-3400. An evangelical ministry stressing traditional family values. They also publish a magazine called *Single Parent Family,* offering support and special encouragement for single parents. Call 1-800-232-6459.
- Social Services. Local offices are usually listed in the "County" section of your telephone directory. See such

listings as "Public Health Services" and "Public Social Services Agency." The many services available include financial aid, food stamps, resources for emergency needs, adult education, day care, and housing.

BUILDING BLOCK #5:

Ask your husband to help.

Do you have a hard time asking your husband for help? If so, why? What is one task he could help you accomplish? In the next twenty-four hours? On a regular basis?

If these and similar questions have been bothering you, decide to have a talk with your husband. Choose the calmest moment of the day when he is most relaxed and likely to be most receptive. Think about what you will say. Use "I" messages rather than make accusations: In other words, resist the temptation to say, "You never help me." Instead, say, "I feel overwhelmed at dinnertime and need some help. What part of the preparation would you like to do?"

Depending on the task, can you accept a result that may be different from the way you would do it?

When will you ask for more help? Today? Tomorrow?

BUILDING BLOCK #6:

Find a Christian counselor.

The following is a list of steps to follow in locating a trustworthy and effective Christian counselor:

- Ask your friends and pastor for referrals. Watch for the same name coming up from different sources.
- Check with several churches for referrals. Again watch for a recurring name. Larger churches in your community will probably have the most developed list.
- Stipulate your need for a counselor who believes the Bible and holds to doctrinal beliefs with which you agree.

- Once you have identified a few counselors, call them and ask for a short interview on the phone. While interviewing them, ask the following:
  — "Will you give me a list of references (pastors or professionals who recommend you)?"
  — "Will you state your credentials and licensing?" Also ask for a disclosure form that details their counseling procedures and philosophy.
  — "Do you have experience in—(the specific issues you are dealing with)?" These may include marriage difficulties, blended family issues, adultery, substance abuse, money problems, pornography, anxiety, physical abuse, eating disorders, low self-esteem, discipline problems, and so forth.

Keep in mind that counselors are not going to fix you. Their role is as facilitator. If you want change to take place, you need to accept responsibility for your own attitudes and behavior and have a willingness to change where indicated. Pursuing the help you need to become a healthy family may take a long-term commitment. Quick therapy is generally a Band-Aid® over a gaping wound.[12]

FOR FURTHER READING:

Do I Have To? Patricia Sprinkle
From One Single Mother to Another, Sandra P. Aldrich
The Marriage Builder, Larry Crabb
Parenting Solo: How to Enjoy Life and Raise Good Kids, Dr. Emil Authelet
Single, But Not Alone, Ellen Weber
Thriving As a Working Woman, Gwen Ellis
The Working Mother's Guide to Sanity, Elsa Houtz
Working Women, Workable Lives: Creative Solutions for Managing Home and Career, Karen Linamen and Linda Holland

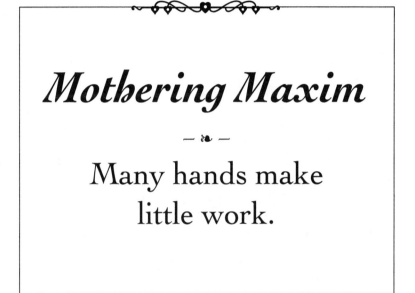

Mothering Maxim

— ❧ —

Many hands make
little work.

Seven

Recreation:

Sometimes I need a break

Eighteen-month-old Scott whimpered as Lynne lifted him from the crib and pressed his feverish forehead to her cheek. She'd been up with him most of the night and knew he needed to see the doctor. He clung to her neck—a hot, sweaty body in his footie jammies—as she dialed the phone number and made an appointment for an hour later. Mentally, she began to rearrange her day.

"Stephen!" she called to her older son. "You need to get dressed. We have to take Scott to the doctor!" Now that he was four, Stephen could at least dress himself, but he'd have to miss preschool this morning. And now she wouldn't be able to do the family bills for Jeff today as she'd promised.

At the doctor's office, Lynne read to Stephen while trying to comfort Scott on her lap. She touched his flushed cheeks and guessed that his temperature was soaring. Sure enough. A few minutes later, the doctor diagnosed another ear infection—his third in six months.

Lynne gratefully took the prescription slip, zipped Scott and Stephen back into their coats, loaded up her diaper bag and purse, and headed back to the car.

When they pulled into the grocery store parking lot, Scott started to cry. "Honey, hang on," she said soothingly. "Mommy's going to get you some medicine." He quieted as she lifted him into her arms and took Stephen's hand as they walked into the store.

"It'll be about twenty minutes," the pharmacist told her. Great. How was she going to keep two little kids happy in the aisles of a grocery store? Her head began to ache. *I can do this,* she told herself calmly.

Forty-five minutes later, Lynne finally arrived back home, made soup for Stephen and coaxed a few bites down Scott, followed by his medicine. At last, she rocked Scott to sleep and settled Stephen down with a video.

Now I can get something done, she thought as she picked up the orders—due yesterday—from last week's Tupperware® party. But as she sat down at the kitchen table with her calculator, she noticed a big mess on the carpet in the next room.

Dog throwup! She jumped up, grabbed a wad of paper towels, hauled out the vacuum, and returned to the mess. But as she flicked the switch, the vacuum hissed and stopped. She recognized that sound . . . a broken belt.

So back to the closet she marched to get a new belt. When she returned to the defunct vacuum, she turned it upside down and plopped down on the floor. Right beside the dog mess.

Hastily, she pulled at the steel belt cover, but it wouldn't budge. Suddenly, it was all too much for her. She had nothing left. Hot tears ran down her face, taking her mascara with them. *Good grief! I can make it through a whole night with a sick child, a doctor's visit and a half-hour delay at the pharmacy, but I fall apart because I can't fix a broken vacuum belt!*

"Mom! The movie's over!" called Stephen from the other room. "Now what do I do?"

"What do *I* do?" Lynne cried. "I need a break!" But no one responded.

ALWAYS ON DUTY

This mom is not alone. Most moms of young children report that it is not a single major crisis that brings them to the edge of breakdown. Rather, it is the constant accumulation of everyday hassles. With no breaks. It's also the constant drive to live up to expectations: "Cleanliness is next to godliness." "Don't put off to tomorrow what you can do today." "Don't play until your work is done." Women hear these ditties from the time they are small children. Added to the list for moms of preschoolers are such condemning prescriptives as: "But your child needs you!"

Even if I'm over at a friend's house having coffee, I can "hear" my children. Even when I'm asleep, I'm still listening for them. There is no time when I am "off duty."

— ❧ —

Day after day, there is no time for me!

— ❧ —

I desperately need time for myself . . . time to just relax, be myself, recharge my battery, so I can make it to the weekend when my husband will be home.

Moms of preschoolers are said to be the most exhausted, fatigued, and worn-out strata of our society. Functioning on little sleep, unbalanced nutrition, little exercise, and frazzled nerves, we're expected to constantly juggle a jumble of balls without ever dropping one or losing our footing.

Often, the cycle of exhaustion intensifies as moms push themselves harder and harder to perform better and better, until they collapse into helpless heaps. "Chronically tired women exhibit sluggishness, impatience, depression, irritability, and emotional outbursts," writes Dolores Curran. "They aren't easy to live with, even with themselves. And they don't like their lives very much. Often the fatigued woman tries to do more than less, feeling that renewed activity will reduce her tiredness."[1]

No kidding! We're worn out! Wrung out!

When I resigned from my management job to be a full-time mom/homemaker, I expected to finally have more time to pray and read, and so forth. Was I ever wrong! Being home full-time with my children means I have less time for myself. I no longer get breaks and no lunch hour to do with as I please!

— ❧ —

The first few weeks after my son was born, I would have given anything to have my old life back again . . . to take a nap on Sunday afternoon, to go camping on the spur of the moment, or go out without worrying about a baby-sitter. I didn't expect such a constant weight of responsibility—with no breaks.

— ❧ —

I know why I went back to work. I needed the rest!

Sucked dry! The unceasing needs, the responsibility, the pressure to be all our children need . . .

EVERYONE BUT MOM

Kids play. Dads channel surf. Even grandmas and grandpas enjoy the whimsical, more carefree stuff of life. But a mom is constantly surrounded by her responsibilities, and that means work, work, work.

But here's the perplexing part: While the need for a break is universally expressed, the habit of taking time for recreation is almost nonexistent. Moms need a break, but they don't take it.

Anne Morrow Lindbergh talks about this need and how a woman gives herself away without taking time for replenishment:

> All her instinct as a woman—the eternal nourisher of children, of men, of society—demands that she give. Her time, her energy, her creativeness drain out into these channels if there is any chance, any leak. Traditionally we are taught, and instinctively we long, to give where it is needed—and immediately. Eternally, woman spills herself away in driblets to the thirsty, seldom being allowed the time, the quiet, the peace, to let the pitcher fill up to the brim.[2]

Sometimes we don't take breaks because we're uncertain about leaving our children.

> *Leaving my children has always been very traumatic. They seem to get thrown off schedule and are extremely clingy when I return.*
>
> — ❧ —
>
> *What if my children need me and I'm not there?!*

Others "break not" because of some belief that it's lazy or selfish to kick back.

> *I don't take breaks and don't realize I need to until I am unkind and unreasonable. Then my husband says, "You need a break." Why can't I sense that before it's too late?*

To this excuse, Dr. Holly Atkinson responds that most women have been reared to believe their needs should come last: "A woman is trained to be self-sacrificing. To get through her list of things to do, she first sacrifices her free time. Then she sacrifices her sleep."[3]

> *I keep thinking I can stay up late to get time for myself. But I'm not as young as I used to be and it just ends up making me more tired and grumpy!*

Moms of preschoolers have a basic, undeniable need to take a break before they break. To come apart before they come apart. To play. To recreate.

RE-CREATION

"Where freedom of play has been lost," writes Jurgen Moltman in *The Theology of Play,* "the world turns into a desert." Too many mothers of preschoolers live a desert life. What is needed is space—both a time and a place—to recreate. To *re-create* who we are and what we have to offer others.

The word *recreate* actually means "to restore, refresh, or create anew" and can mean "to restore in body or mind especially after work, by play, amusement or relaxation." What moms of young children need is re-creation!

Re-creation makes us better.

A recent *McCall's* survey reports that women are two to four times more likely than men to suffer from nightmares, upset stomachs, and feelings of being overwhelmed and depressed.

Eighty-three percent of the women surveyed feel pressure to be the best in everything they do.

Interestingly, laughter and leisure combine to alleviate stress and its ill-effects. When Norman Cousins faced a serious illness, he used the therapy of laughter in his recovery. Ten-minute daily doses of *Candid Camera* and *The Marx Brothers* taken from his hospital bed eased his pain and helped him to sleep well.

Re-creation renews us. "Leisure . . . is a point of contact with reality and a catalyst for new experiences, new people, and new places," writes Tim Hansel in his book, *When I Relax, I Feel Guilty.* "It is the time when the gift of wholeness again becomes a hope and a possibility."[4]

Re-creation makes us better moms.

Who among us doesn't want to be a better mom? We weigh our efforts and wonder how to improve our impact on our kids. A study at the universities of Utah and Wisconsin reveals that stress (including daily maternal hassles) causes more interference in the relationship between a mother and her child than a job.[5]

It is really nice to get out without the children and talk to people my age or just do something I want without children to look after. When I come back home, after time by myself, I feel better about myself and my children. It feels like I'm back on track with my kids as far as patience and understanding.

When we take a break to make ourselves better, we become better moms. As Dolores Curran puts it, "Taking a break is not selfish but self-preserving."[6] And pastor's wife, Denise Turner, has also learned this truth for herself: "A long time passed before I realized the ability to enjoy my children is closely dependent upon the amount of time I am spending having fun with my husband and having fun by myself."[7]

The fact is that after caring for our own needs a bit, we're better equipped to meet the needs of those who depend upon us.

I'm at my most self-disciplined and patient best when I have chosen time for prayer, a walk, and some reading in the morning.

— ❧ —

My husband and I hadn't been out alone together for almost a year. On our big night out we went shopping for a mattress. We were so excited—we had a blast!

Taking time for recreation communicates to others, our families especially, that we recognize the value of taking care of ourselves. So how do we learn to take a break and enjoy the benefits it offers?

PLAY SCHOOL

Most of us have to learn how to play. We figured it out as children, of course, but as we head into our adult years, we outgrow the habit of playing, just as we outgrow items of clothing. As adults, play means getting in touch with the childlikeness we've left behind. Several ingredients go into play. We can learn to enjoy them individually or in combination.

Learn to Laugh

When we can laugh at life and at ourselves as we muddle through it, we are happier, saner, and even more physically fit. Laughter eases strain and relaxes tension. According to some studies, it exercises the abdomen, increases circulation, and improves muscle tone. It's been said that laughing heartily several times a day has the same benefits as ten minutes of vigorous exercise. So let's get started!

I awoke one morning to find my children sitting in a mound of Cheerios® on the floor. They were so thrilled about fixing breakfast—I had to laugh!

Laughing at ourselves takes the sting out of our mistakes as well as those things we simply can't control. Since we have to live with ourselves, we might as well be good company. Humor also helps us a grip on situations where we tend to lose our temper.

"The mother who can laugh at herself, with her children, and at the impossible situations of life, is far ahead on the road to personal control," write Grace Ketterman and Pat Holt in their book, *When You Feel Like Screaming*. "Having the wisdom to step back and see the humor . . . helps (us) gain control."[8]

Laughter also gives us *perspective*.

Laughter is contagious. Someone once said, "Smile awhile and while you smile, another smiles and soon there are miles and miles of smiles because you smiled." But it was William Arthur Ward who put it all in a nutshell when he wrote: "A keen sense of humor helps us overlook the unbecoming, to understand the unconventional, to tolerate the unpleasant, to overcome the unexpected, and to outlast the unbearable."[9]

Lighten Up

What's the big deal? Why do we take so many things so seriously when they aren't that important? For example, we need to ask ourselves what's more important—tucking a happy, grubby child into bed or a clean, cranky one?

We need to bring spontaneity back into our routine occasionally. We assume that a trip outside the front door requires the accompaniment of armloads of equipment. But does it really? What would happen if we had only one diaper, some wipes, and a bottle of juice in our possession at any given moment? What if—instead of fretting over the pile of Legos® littering our living room floor—we got down among them and saw life from the perspective of a two-year-old? Did you ever notice how many exciting stimuli lie just six inches off the floor? How about breaking your schedule for some unplanned fun? What if—on a clear summer night—you woke your child and took her stargazing?

Where's the fun? I thought mothering would be fun. Instead, it's filled with one drudgery after another.

I got so tired of being late during the days of potty-training. So I put the potty chair in the minivan and strapped my little guy in!

Re-creation requires spontaneity. Don't put your life on hold during these days filled with opportunities to make memories with your little ones.

Embrace fun wherever and whenever it comes, and enter into it wholly. "We ought to treat fun reverently," writes *New York Times* reporter Suzanne Britt Jordan. "It is a mystery. It cannot be caught like a virus. It cannot be trapped like an animal. When it does come in, on little dancing feet, you probably won't be expecting it. In fact, I bet it comes when you're doing your duty or your work. It may even come on a Tuesday."[10]

Slow Down

What's the hurry? In his book, *The Hurried Child*, David Elkind cautions us to slow down our lives and our mothering.

We're racing ourselves and our children ahead past the very work of play they need to do in childhood.

Six-month-old babies are learning to sit, not run. Eighteen-month-olds move away from Mom and then back again every few minutes as they journey out to explore their worlds, while making sure she's close by. Three-year-olds want to touch, see, and do everything all by themselves and are frustrated if they can't.

Childhood comes with its specific tasks of accomplishment. Among them is play. In fact, a child's work *is* play. Through play, children internalize their personhood, sexuality, and understanding about life. When we forget either our children's need to play or our own, we forfeit the joy of living life as it was intended to be lived.

Slow down. Savor where you are. Believe it or not, this season shall pass. Quickly.

PHYSICAL FITNESS FUN

Doctors, psychologists, and other experts knowingly tout the benefits of physical fitness on general well-being. Bottom-line, when we're out of shape, we don't feel good and tire easily. In short, we're wretched to live with!

The break many moms need is simply a walk around the block to feel the fresh air and get the blood flowing. Some need better nutrition — something other than leftover peanut-butter-and-jelly sandwiches and Cheerios.

I never get any exercise. And my exhaustion overcomes my enthusiasm.

— ❧ —

I used to play tennis and be active, but now I'm out of shape.

And others need to lie down for a half-hour nap each day. All these ingredients add up to physical fitness.

While it's sometimes next to impossible to get that needed break, you can learn to take advantage of odd moments here and there. Get up early and go for a jog while your husband is home. Trade kids with a friend and take a walk in your neighborhood.

Listen to a cassette or pray while you pound the pavement. Head off to your local YWCA or city recreation center for a workout. Most offer day-care facilities by the hour. New moms in San Mateo, California, have started "strollerobics," exercise routines done in a class with their babies in strollers![11] The message is—be creative. Where there's a will, you *will* find a way.

Need to cultivate better nutritional habits? Diet with some pals. "Just say no to one temptation a day. Don't eat leftovers off the children's plates. Give up sugar for one weekend. Check out the fat grams for one meal. Stop snacking. Include more fruits and vegetables in the family menu. (The recommended quota is five servings a day.) Play a game with the children of counting them up, starting with juice at breakfast. Enlist the children's help in peeling oranges or tearing lettuce. Often when a child becomes a part-time chef, he or she will be more interested in tasting new creations.

Be intentional about getting more rest. When you lay your little one down for a nap, lie down yourself. If your child has outgrown naps, maintain the regular quiet time and use that to lie down together and read. No, you won't get the next load of wash folded, but you might be much easier to live with!

For many of us with overcrowded schedules, physical fitness is one of the first things to go. We figure no one will notice. Wrong. Whether or not the lack of love for our bodies shows on the outside, the inside suffers. And eventually, the damage will be demonstrated in the form of impatience, irritability, and general grouchiness. If a woman doesn't feel good about herself, she's less likely to treat others with goodness.

Getting into shape often takes discipline and determination, but the results are worthwhile and the process—once underway—can be fun. A bonus: Exercise is addictive. Some advice? Just do it!

FEED YOUR SPIRIT

During the days when we are giving on demand, we need a constant source of nourishment for ourselves as well.

Psalm 42:1–4 provides a mental picture of the many moms who'd love to spend time with God but can't seem to fit it into their hectic days: "As the deer pants for streams of water, so my soul pants for you, O God. My soul thirsts for God, for the living God. When can I go and meet with God?"

There are many days when our spirits feel parched and we wonder when—or if—we'll ever "meet with God" again. Even getting to church once a week is often difficult.

Instead of waiting to go to the "house of the Lord," why not invite him to your house? Sit down during a child's naptime and read a few verses from the gospel of John. Use a meal-time blessing to really pray about what's happened that day. Leave your Bible open on the table and grab a phrase from one of the psalms as you walk by. Graze on Scripture morsels throughout the day from a flipbook on the kitchen counter. Listen to a tape of the New Testament in the car. Take a prayer walk through the neighborhood and talk to God about the details of your day.

When you think of taking a break, include a practice that will feed your spirit.

FOCUS ON FUN

Learn to laugh. Lighten up with spontaneity. Slow down. Get in shape. Feed your spirit. Be intentional about including fun in life.

Re-creation happens when we commit ourselves to focusing on fun, both for ourselves and for our family.

In my job before I had children, I got in the habit of only doing what was on my Daytimer. If it wasn't there, I didn't do it. Having fun is never written there now.

Mom Fun

Moms need something that is enjoyable for themselves alone, not to be shared with children or other family members. Plan

A toy closet is my escape. I feel like a kid for a few moments, escaping and hiding from everyone.

creatively to take a break by yourself. It might be only "Five Minutes of Peace," carved out of your own wild world.

Your "peaceful moment" might even come during a quick trip to the supermarket or while running an errand. One mom describes her habit of "Wal-Marting":

> Wal-Marting goes something like this: My day has gotten progressively worse. Any slight deviation from routine sets off my temper. My children seem particularly fussy. We run out of juice midday. The kitten keeps using the couch as a scratching post. Two unexpected bills come in the mail, and I get four phone calls during naptime. I can hardly wait for my husband to get home from work. As he walks through the door and asks me how my day has been, I explain that I am in need of some alone time. He says he'll see me later. I hop in the car and head to Wal-Mart.[12]

Your time alone might come through a scheduled breakaway. Many moms plan regular times for themselves. A craft or cooking class. A workout. A walk. A night out with the girls.

Ask your husband for help, or if you're single, swap kids with another single mom. But deliberately set aside time for renewal. Then take action to ensure that you use it. You'll find refreshment both in the anticipation and in the experience itself.

I agree to play hide-and-seek with the kids—they hide, and I get all the peace I want whenever I want until I choose to find them!

— ❧ —

We have a barn, horses, and a lot of hay bales. When I need some peace, I announce that I need to go out and restack the hay, but I really just go and sit on them. I can usually get thirty minutes out of this excuse and [my husband] never says anything to me about the messy barn!

Family Fun

Dolores Curran, in her book *Traits of a Healthy Family,* lists a sense of play and humor as an important ingredient of a happy, balanced family. Some moms already know that family fun matters.

"Most middle-class Americans tend to worship their work, to work at their play, and to play at their worship," writes Gordon Dahl. "Their relationships disintegrate faster than they can keep them in repair, and their lifestyles resemble a cast of characters in search of a plot."[13]

As moms, we need to learn to make time for family fun. If we don't *plan* to play, it usually won't happen.

My son, to be kind to me one day, helped me with several chores. We did laundry together, swept floors, put away toys, and on and on. Later that day, he said that we did everything but we hadn't had any time for fun. My goals were met, but my son wanted my time and laughter more than anything. Now we set aside a day just for the "fun" stuff.

Here are several suggestions for focused family fun:

- *Hold a family forum.* Let each family member select a fun activity for the month. Set the tone by being enthusiastic about the prospect. Include yourself in the decision-making process. You, too, should take a turn at creating fun.
- *View your family members as toys.* Instead of looking for pastimes that cost money or purchasing amusements, think of the folks around you as a free source of fun.
- *Celebrate the daily as well as the sensational.* "Celebration brings joy into life," writes Richard Foster in his book, *Celebration of Discipline,* "and joy makes us strong."[14] Make celebration a part of your family.

  Designate a dinner plate as a "Very Special Person Plate" and serve a meal on it to a family member in honor of an achievement or special occasion. Pull out all the stops on birthdays with balloons, homemade cards, birthday serenades at the exact moment of birth, and birthday crowns. Underline the value of each person in your family by singling out special days and moments to celebrate.

- *Keep traditions.* Every family has a few rituals they have "always" observed. Combine the memorable ones from your background with some from your husband's background, and then invent some new ones. Rituals offer meaning, predictability, and a heritage of values.

Moms of preschoolers are among the most needy when it comes to recreation. But we need to cultivate the habits of learning to laugh, lightening up, slowing down, and having fun. Take a break . . . before you break! ❧

BUILDING BLOCKS

BUILDING BLOCK #1:

Build a laugh library.

Keep bone-ticklers on hand:

- Collections of cartoons or jokes or videos that make you laugh, such as *Baby Blues, Family Circus,* or *Calvin and Hobbes,* or reruns of *Candid Camera* or favorite home videos.
- Good reading material, such as:

Stick a Geranium in Your Hat and Be Happy! by Barbara Johnson

Cracked Pots by Patsy Clairmont

Motherhood: The Second Oldest Profession by Erma Bombeck

Worms in My Tea by Becky Freeman and Ruthie Arnold

BUILDING BLOCK #2:

Laugh off stress.

• *Cultivate a smile habit.* Your facial expression is contagious, so smile to yourself, smile at your kids, and smile at others—at stoplights, in the mall, or anywhere.

When you wear a smile across your face, it's not as easy to feel growly and grouchy.

• *Learn to laugh.* Laughter can help fight stress and promote healing. Here's how to laugh off stress:

1. Try to see the humor in the situations around you.
2. Imagine how a child might see your situation.
3. Take your job seriously and yourself lightly.
4. Be spontaneous. Loosen up and lighten up.
5. Play . . . with kids, dogs, cats, kites, whatever.
6. When in doubt, go for the goofy.
7. Browse the comedy aisle at the video store.
8. Go out to a comedy club.
9. Spend time with friends who make you chuckle.[15]

BUILDING BLOCK #3:

Try twenty-three ways to lighten up.

When his son was getting ready to begin college life, H. Jackson Brown jotted down a few words of wisdom to send with him. Brown didn't know then that all over America people would take his advice to heart. Here are twenty-three of the 511 tips from his best-selling *Life's Little Instruction Book:*

  3. Watch a sunrise.
10. Learn to play a musical instrument.
11. Sing in the shower.
40. Never refuse homemade brownies.
69. Whistle.

144. Take someone bowling.
150. Sing in a choir.
152. Fly Old Glory on the Fourth of July.
182. Be romantic.
244. Buy a bird feeder and place it where it can be seen from your kitchen window.
246. Wave at children on school buses.
261. Take family vacations.
267. Lie on your back and look at the stars.
330. Rekindle old friendships.
337. Reread your favorite book.
344. Patronize drugstores with soda fountains.
345. Try everything offered by supermarket food demonstrators.
347. Never waste an opportunity to tell someone you love them.
376. Save an evening a week for just you and your spouse.
402. Begin each day with your favorite music.
443. Laugh a lot.
477. Give thanks before every meal.
510. Count your blessings.[16]

BUILDING BLOCK #4:

Get in shape.

Here's a Six-Week Starter Program that will help you reduce stress and tension and have you looking and feeling better fast.

- *Weeks 1, 2, and 3:* Walk outside, or get on your exercycle, stair-climber, or treadmill for fifteen minutes, three times a week.
  - Don't worry about distance or pace; focus solely on getting in fifteen minutes of exercise time.

— Move your legs fast enough to increase your breathing rate, but not so fast that you become breathless. Maintain a *steady* pace where you're comfortable throughout your exercise period.

— Ideal times to exercise are before breakfast or before dinner. (Indoor exercisers can watch TV or read while they exercise.)

- *Week 4:* Exercise for twenty minutes, three times.
- *Week 5:* Exercise for twenty-five minutes, three times.
- *Week 6:* Exercise for thirty minutes, three times.

After week 6, you can either gradually increase time to forty-five or sixty minutes; or you can gradually increase your pace within the thirty-minute time frame.

Walkers can alternate brisk walking with *slow* jogging (fast jogging and running increase your risk for injury).

Indoor exercisers can increase the tension on their exercise equipment.

Note: If you're trying to lose excess weight, consider getting a minimum of thirty-five minutes of brisk exercise *every* day.

BUILDING BLOCK #5:

Sneak in a workout.

If you're a new mom with little time on your hands, use these ideas to help snatch a quick exercise session:

- While your tot naps, rake leaves, shovel snow, sweep the driveway, or do other calorie-burning yardwork with a monitor close at hand.
- Join a health club that provides child care while moms work out.
- Take your baby on long walks in the stroller, or buy a three-wheeled jog stroller.
- Buy a baby tote for biking.

- Design a plan with another new mom who wants to work out. She keeps the babies for an hour while you exercise; then you keep them while she works out.
- Hide your husband's golf clubs on the weekend so you can step out and exercise while he keeps the kids for an hour or two.
- Hire a baby-sitter while you work out—a healthy body and less-stressed mind is worth the few bucks.
- Exercise to a TV workout show or rent your favorite celebrity's workout video to use while baby naps.[17]

BUILDING BLOCK #6:

Keep up appearances.

Setting aside the time to fix your hair and makeup isn't always easy with small children underfoot, but once done, it goes a long way toward making your days go more smoothly.

Here are some beautiful ideas for at-home maintenance:

- As the song says, "Everybody's beautiful" in her own way, so think positively when you look into the mirror. Stand up straight and tighten your abdominals—this forces you into an upright position and into a more positive attitude. Try a little of the unabashed admiration that your toddler uses when he looks at himself in the mirror. Do not be preoccupied with your flaws.
- Find a flattering hairstyle, then maintain it.
- Spend a little time planning your outfits. Get rid of the ratty garments from your closet so that you're not tempted to wear them.
- Don't abandon the little self-pampering luxuries you enjoyed before you had kids. Put someone else in charge of the real world while you take time out for a bubble bath. Then give yourself a manicure and pedicure, tweeze your eyebrows, and condition your hair. Treat yourself to a fa-

cial mask. Put wet teabags over your eyes to remove puffiness.

- Invite a friend over and give each other a make-over. Solicit feedback on a potential new hairdo or make-up approach. These grooming sessions still serve a social function that didn't end with adolescent slumber parties!

- If you love to keep up with fashion trends, read women's magazines for new hair and makeup techniques and fashion ideas. But read with caution: Make sure you only come away with new ideas and techniques; leave the idealized standards of perfection for the recycle bin. Remember the words of Abe Lincoln upon overhearing someone remark that he was a "common-looking man": "Friend, the Lord prefers common-looking people. That is the reason he makes so many of them."[18]

BUILDING BLOCK #7:

Use this fitness checklist.

The following habits will help create a healthy lifestyle:

- Don't skip breakfast.
- Drink eight glasses of water a day.
- Exercise at least three times a week.
- Eat a healthy diet, including:
  — Five servings of vegetables or fruits every day.
  — Iron- and calcium-rich foods such as lean meats and green, leafy vegetables, including a vitamin supplement if necessary.
  — Foods low in fat, high in protein and carbohydrates.
- Get some fresh air daily.
- Carve out a sliver of quiet or alone time.
- Get adequate rest even if that means choosing to take a quick nap when your child rests instead of cleaning the living room.

BUILDING BLOCK #8:

Take Bible bites.

Come to me, all you who are weary and burdened, and I will give you rest. Take my yoke upon you and learn from me, for I am gentle and humble in heart, and you will find rest for your souls. For my yoke is easy and my burden is light. (Matt. 11:28–30).

A happy heart makes the face cheerful, but heartache crushes the spirit (Prov. 15:13).

A cheerful heart is good medicine, but a crushed spirit dries up the bones (Prov. 17:22).

He settles the barren woman in her home as a happy mother of children (Ps. 113:9).

Very early in the morning, while it was still dark, Jesus got up, left the house and went off to a solitary place, where he prayed (Mark 1:35).

BUILDING BLOCK #9:

Plan a fun campaign.

Here are some ideas to get intentional about having fun:

- Once in awhile, write a note to excuse your child from preschool to play with his mom. Then plan a special activity, like a picnic in the park. Swing on the swings together.
- Expose yourself to new people and places. Take a day trip to an ethnic neighborhood. Read up on the culture and customs of other countries. Dine at ethnic eateries.
- Develop a hobby. Think back over your life to the hobbies of your childhood. Pull out the stamp collection or the crafts from camp that excited you. Sign up for a class in pottery, painting, or woodworking at a community college. Consider joining a book club that reads and re-

views current best-sellers in a small group atmosphere. Get outdoors through gardening. Pick up some gourmet skills in a cooking class.

FOR FURTHER READING:

Finding Time for Family Fun, Gwen Weising
Food for Life, Pamela Smith, R.D.
Let's Make a Memory, Shirley Dobson and Gloria Gaither
Little House on the Freeway, Tim Kimmel
Mother's Survival Manual Series, Kathy Peel and Joy Mahaffey
Table Talk, Mimi Wilson and Mary Beth Lagerborg
When I Relax, I Feel Guilty, Tim Hansel
When You Feel Like Screaming, Pat Holt and Grace Ketterman

Mothering Maxim

— ❧ —

If Mama ain't happy,
ain't nobody happy.

Eight

Perspective:
Sometimes I lose my focus

Debbie stood at the kitchen sink, gazing out the window and daydreaming about the time when the kids would be grown and she would live in a house without clutter. Then, snapping back to reality, she remembered the water gushing from the faucet and began rinsing the breakfast dishes. Next, she wiped milk stains and sticky crumbs from the counter and swept the floor. Glancing into the family room, she saw her next task looming before her—cleaning the carpet littered with puzzle pieces, a plastic tea set, clothes, and crayons.

Just then she felt a tug on her jeans and looked down.

"Mommy, can you read to me?" four-year-old Shannon pleaded, clutching her favorite book, *Goodnight Moon*. Debbie had read that book to Shannon hundreds of times in the past few weeks.

"Not now, honey." Debbie sighed. "Maybe later."

Shannon whined and then collapsed at her mother's feet, gluing Debbie in place.

"Shannon! Can't you see that Mommy is very busy today? I have to finish cleaning the kitchen, do the laundry, go to the store, and finish writing those thank-you notes for the presents we got when Meagan was born! And now you've made a huge mess in the family room, and I have to clean that up too!"

"But Mommy—the kitchen *is* clean! And you always do laundry . . . and the carpet doesn't look messy to me. . . ." Shannon pleaded.

"Not now, Shannon. Maybe later," Debbie firmly repeated as she pried the child's arms from her legs and marched to the washing machine. She had only a few towels to fold, but Debbie wasn't one to let them sit.

The phone rang. It was her dear friend and former co-worker, Beth. After chatting about old times for about fifteen minutes, Debbie went to check on napping Meagan. Good, still asleep.

But where had Shannon taken herself? Peeking around the corner into her daughter's bedroom, Debbie found Shannon sitting in her pint-sized rocking chair, holding a book and facing a row of attentive stuffed animals. They were arranged audience-style and gave the appearance of applauding fans before a great talent.

"In the great, green room, there was a telephone and a red balloon and a picture of a cow jumping over the moon. And there were three little bears sitting on chairs. . . ." Shannon began "reading" from *Goodnight Moon,* mimicking her mother's intonations.

Suddenly she snapped the book shut and announced to her eager audience, "I forgot. I don't have time to read today! I have too much to do!" Rising quickly from her rocker, she marched over to a doll baby, picked her up, and then plopped her down in a playpen. "No, I can't read to you now. Maybe later. And don't ask me again! Can't you see I am busy?!"

Debbie pulled herself back around the corner, leaned against the hall wall, and pondered the role-play she'd just observed. *Ouch! Is that really how Shannon sees me? From the mouth of a four-year-old . . .*

I guess I sometimes forget what's important and lose my focus, she realized.

ANOTHER PERSPECTIVE

Not now, maybe later. It's tough to hear that familiar mother-to-child answer and not feel a few pangs of guilt, isn't it? But this chapter isn't about guilt. It's about a larger struggle that we face day in and day out. The struggle to learn to cope with our busyness and find focus, or perspective. The struggle to balance the urgent and the important. The struggle to recognize our choices and make them with wisdom. So that we're less likely to have regrets or feel guilty.

What do we mean by "perspective"? Perspective is the ability to stand between yesterday and tomorrow and understand how and where today fits in. As the mothers of young children seeking to discover how our "todays" fit into our lifetime roles as women, we have to stand back and get a larger view of the whole of life. We have to identify some goals that transcend today and then remember what we're aiming toward.

Writer Annie Dillard hit upon this angle while staying in a friend's wilderness cabin. One day while attempting to chop some wood, she thought as she struggled, "What I did was less like splitting wood than chipping flints ... [until I discovered] you aim at the chopping block, not at the wood; then you split the wood, instead of chipping it. You cannot do the job cleanly unless you treat the wood as the transparent means to an end, aiming past it."[1]

Perspective means looking beyond the moment with a view toward the whole of life. And moms of preschoolers need perspective as they move through days in which the goal of a clean house can take precedence over tickle-wars, and completing a to-do list may win out over laptime. We need to recognize the difference between "chipping flints" and "splitting wood."

Living with perspective is difficult at any stage of life. The present is so demanding that it takes on meaning of its own, separate from its rightful place in the context of forever. But for the mother of preschoolers, several mothering myths worm their way into our thinking and distort our focus.

MOTHERING MYTHS AND REALITY

We've swallowed certain mothering myths as truths, unaware that it is falsehood that directs much of our thinking as well as our actions. As a result, we often forget why we're doing what we're doing and what really matters in the long run.

Following are four myths coupled with their corresponding realities. Read carefully to see where you might be misled in what motivates your mothering.

Myth #1: If you control everything, life works.

Reality: You can't control everything.
You have to go with the flow.

We tend to believe that we should be in control at every moment, and that if we are, all the big and little things of life will run smoothly.

Ha! That's like a dream . . . and then we get up in the morning and face reality.

Exactly. The myth that we can make life work by being in control gives way to the reality that most of life is beyond our control. Trying to take charge of all events in life only leads to frustration and despair.

I'm surprised I get so upset about unimportant things . . . like a spilled drink.

— ❧ —

An unexpected visitor drops by and I'm so embarrassed by the exposure of my lack of orderliness.

— ❧ —

The hardest part of being a mother is not being able to control what another human being does.

The reality is that life has a life of its own. Take children, for instance. Babies spit up on you just as you're ready to walk out the door. Toddlers wet their training pants three weeks after you thought they'd mastered toilet-training. Kindergartners shyly hang back from their mothers on the first day of school, even though they've been impatiently checking off the days on a calendar for the past month.

Besides children, there is the everyday stuff of life that refuses our commands. Cars stall in traffic. Lines are long at the store. Three bills arrive on the same day. A filling breaks in a tooth. The milk spoils. A button pops off a shirt.

How do we handle the shattering of this myth of control? With a strong dose of practical action.

• *Relinquish control.* The Serenity Prayer, popular for overcoming many addictions, also speaks powerfully to the world of the mother of preschoolers. In those unforgettable words of Reinhold Neibuhr:

> God, grant me the serenity to accept what cannot be
> changed,
> Courage to change what should be changed,
> And the wisdom to know the difference.

Moms who give over control to God report peace and rest.

Deal with the myth that life can be controlled before you lose your perspective and sanity. Relinquish your attempts to control life.

• *Respond only to the responsibility you've been given.* So many of us borrow burdens from others. We decide we're responsible for a friend's happiness, for a child's health, for a husband's fulfillment.

Dr. Marianne Neifert, otherwise known as "Dr. Mom," admits candidly, "I can say: God didn't put all that stuff in my sack. When I looked inside, I saw my ambition, need for other people's approval, perfectionism. Those things were put there by me. That's why my sack was too heavy."[2]

> *God has taught me to wait on him as our military orders changed six times; as my husband decided to find work outside of the military; and as we lived in a state of limbo. All of this is very much against my nature. I am a planner, goal-oriented, compulsive organizer, and perfectionist.*

Along these same lines, A. J. Russell, in his book *God Calling,* suggests that stress results from carrying two days' burdens in one day. His words echo those of Jesus: "Therefore do not worry about tomorrow, for tomorrow will worry about itself. Each day has enough trouble of its own" (Matt. 6:34).

• *Humor helps.* When the myth that we can control life around us shatters, humor helps. Try these lines:

God put me on earth to accomplish a certain number of
    things. Right now I am so far behind, I will never die.

Life is tough . . . and then you die.

Just when you thought you were winning the rat race,
    along come faster rats.

Learn to smile at your inability to control. Humor eases our
    hurts or frustrations as we admit our humanity!

Okay. Are you ready to shatter another myth?

Myth #2: I should do it all right and all right now.

Reality: I can't do it all, but I can do what's important.

Our expectations for ourselves and what we should be accomplishing are astronomically high and unrealistic. We've moved past the Supermom syndrome and climbed atop a pedestal of perfection. We assume that we should be able to do it all right and all right *now!*

Right? Wrong.

"As challenges keep coming," Erma Bombeck once said, "mothers realize they can't possibly keep pace or they'll wind up comatose in the kitchen sink."

I often become overly concerned with the details of everyday life and forget my place in the big picture.

— ≈ —

Reality showed me I cannot be Supermom. The important thing is to leave a legacy and lead my children to God. The dishes can wait.

— ≈ —

I have to remember that I am a home-maker, not a house-keeper.

We can fight against this second myth by taking deliberate steps to define and embrace what really matters in life.

• *Keep the main thing the main thing.* In his book *First Things First,* Stephen Covey challenges his readers to define what really matters: "The main thing is to keep the main thing . . . the main thing!" Covey stresses that we must intentionally commit ourselves to what is important, or we will be committing ourselves to what is unimportant.

For moms of preschoolers, perspective comes as we define what really matters in mothering.

What really matters to you as a mom? A clean home or a kind heart? Your children's habits or their values?

> *I need to be flexible. Trying to stick to my own agenda causes eighty percent of our family's hassles.*

Their attitudes and actions or their appearance? Perspective is restored when we define for ourselves just what it is that we're trying to accomplish as mothers.

• *Allocate the investment of your time and energy based on the "main thing."* This myth of doing it all right and doing it all right *now* leads us to pay too much attention to the niggling little details of life. When we define for ourselves what really matters, we can then use such a definition as a measuring stick of our activities. Where are we spending our energies?

> *I find myself frustrated with my little boy because he demands too much of my attention while I'm trying to get dinner together or fold laundry or whatever. So I try to get him involved in other activities, but he feels that he is being snubbed, so he decides to bring some sand in from outside or climb up and pound on the computer. Before I know it, I'm in a power struggle with him, all because I seem to think that having dinner ready fifteen minutes earlier is more important that sitting with him during a time of day when he is less able to control his impulses. It is times like these that I need to step back and remind myself of what the priorities are.*

Admittedly, there are times when it's tough to know whether or not an issue falls under "the main thing" or not.

> *Just when I think it's "okay" to go through the day in sweats, wear only lipstick or no makeup, and let the house look less than perfect while I spend time nurturing and playing with my children (who won't be children forever) ... and that it's okay not to look perfect (flat stomach, pre-pregnant weight, hair curled), my husband returns home from work with a comment about the house being a mess or dinner not being on the table or "What did you do all day and what's wrong with your hair?"*

Even after the obvious need to communicate and agree upon values with your husband is met, ticklish spots remain. In such moments, ask yourself: "Will it matter in five years?" and "What would happen if I ignored this issue?" Such questions provide the parameters we need to keep our focus.

Here's a third mothering myth. See if you can relate.

Myth #3: The best way to make it through mothering is to grin and bear it until it gets better.

Reality: Enjoy today. Make the most of life's irretrievable moments . . . now.

How much of mothering we miss because our focus is simply on making it through! Sure, we all seethe in the face of well-intentioned advice from kindly grandmothers in grocery stores who tell us (as we wrestle with three cranky kids in the checkout line), "These are the best days of your life! Enjoy them because they pass so quickly!"

"Not quickly enough," we mutter under our breath.

But these women do have a point. One that comes with the wisdom of their years. The stage of mothering young children is a *stage*. It only *feels* like an era! And it will pass. It will not last forever. It will end one day.

When we accept the myth that the best we can do is to simply "grin and bear it," we miss out on what mothering can mean. While we're wishing ourselves into the next season, we miss the good stuff that's happening now. This myth is shattered when we deliberately determine to make the most of life's irretrievable moments.

Here's how:

• *Live in the present.* How quickly we push past today to reach tomorrow!

> First I was dying to finish high school
> and start college.
> And then I was dying to finish
> college and start working.

And then I was dying to marry
and have children.
And then I was dying for my children
to grow old enough for school
so I could return to work.
And then I was dying to retire.
And now, I am
dying . . .
And suddenly I realize I forgot to live.

—Anonymous

Today you are indispensably valuable in the life of someone else!

A hundred years from now . . . it will not matter what my bank account was, the sort of house I lived in, or the kind of car I drove. . . but the world may be different because I was important in the life of a child.

—Anonymous

This week you have the opportunity to get on the floor and build block towers. This is the season when you are invited to read, to play, to imagine, to dream! Your lap is the "favorite-est place to be." Your smile is more valuable than money. Your words mean more than those on the television, in a magazine, or in a classroom. Savor the moments of this season that will never come around again.

Yesterday is history.
Tomorrow is a mystery.
Today is a gift.
That's why we call it "The Present."

—Anonymous

We tend to believe that life will get better when, really, it just gets different. If the grass looks greener on the other side of your fence, it may be because you're not investing your time and energy in your own grass. Live in the present.

• *Enjoy the little things.* Treasure each moment. Like precious stones, they are yours to touch, appreciate, and store in your heart to ponder and relive.

> For life is short, the years rush past.
> A little boy grows up so fast.
> No longer is he at your side,
> His precious secrets to confide.
> The picture books are put away.
> There are no more games to play.
> No goodnight kiss, no prayers to hear—
> That all belongs to yesteryear.
> My hands once busy now lie still.
> The days are long and hard to fill.
> I wish I might go back and do
> The little things you asked me to.

> —Anonymous

One last mothering myth tends to rob us of our mothering perspective.

Myth #4: Mothering is serious business and the lives of your children are at stake at every moment.

*Reality: Lighten up. Children are resilient.
Handle them with honesty and humor.*

Fear obscures perspective. Focusing on the worst case scenario, the unimaginable horror of what even remotely might lie ahead, our fears leap out of all proportion and blur our vision of reality.

If I don't read to my young children enough, I've heard that they'll never be admitted to the college of their choice. And what about fevers? If I don't take care of my baby's high fever, I just learned that her permanent teeth could come in permanently yellowed!

And our fears multiply. "Be sure to scrub your cutting board in hot soapy water every time you use it, or you could infect your entire family with the bacteria in the raw chicken you cut up." "If you let your child cry for even a few minutes, you will endanger the bonding process, and studies show that a disruption in bonding is often the cause of criminal behavior later in life."

While mothering is crucial and good mothering even more valuable, falling victim to the fear of ruining our children with a single mistake is unrealistic. Fight off this myth by recognizing that children are resilient.

• *Honor your children with honesty.* When you make a mistake, learn to forgive yourself and let go of your failure. Refuse to pack up your guilt and carry it with you. Say you're sorry and move on. When your child asks a question, tell her the truth. Children do not expect their mothers to be perfect—unless we have taught them to expect perfection. They will respond with respect when inadequacies are shared appropriately.

• *Handle your children with humor.* In his book, *The Strong Family*, Chuck Swindoll warns us to avoid a pessimistic outlook.

> Call me crazy if you like (you won't be the first), but I am more convinced than ever that attitudes shape just about everything we do. Not facts, not a group of so-called authorities. Not some big, thick book spelling the demise of civilization . . . but attitudes.[3]

Lighten up and laugh at yourself. Children most often respond to a light touch, not the heavy hand. Teach them to laugh at themselves as well. Make "OOPS!" the password of your home. Find something extra in the ordinary to celebrate. Take mothering just a little bit less seriously and watch how you blossom—and your children along with you!

Four myths of mothering. If we believe them and what they stand for, we're sure to lose our focus. But when we replace them with reality, perspective returns.

A PERSPECTIVE OF CHOICE

One of the most challenging aspects of mothering is the challenge of choices. How do I know if I can/should go through delivery without medication? Should I go back to work after the baby is born? What philosophy of discipline will work best for my child? How do I choose a school or day care program? And what about me? How and when should I take time for myself? What really matters in the long run?

Perspective offers the wisdom needed to make such choices on a daily basis. Perspective is fitting today in between yesterday and tomorrow. It's understanding that today has value as it grows out of yesterday and as it shapes tomorrow. Perspective gives mothers of preschoolers the ability to endure the drudgery and demands of today because that attention prepares our children for the future.

Various descriptions have been used to explain the choice-making dilemma faced by mothers.

What are your priorities?

Perspective for choice-making is said to be simplified when you identify your priorities. But the process may not be as clear or simple as it sounds. If your priority is to bring up a healthy, happy, well-adjusted child, you'll stay home from work to attend to his nurturing needs. Authorities everywhere agree that the mother is the single-most important influence on the development of a child. Clear priority, simple choice. Right?

Maybe . . . except when you also need to work in order to put food on the table. Few children are happy and well-adjusted when they aren't fed.

Your husband may also be a priority. He wants you to spend more time alone with him. But your baby is sick and crying for you. What are you supposed to do? Which one gets top priority?

Whose need do you put first?

You may recognize a priority for giving yourself a break and an opportunity for growth now and then in order to be fresh and effective as a mom. But what do you do when your toddler comes down with a cold the night of your first seminar, or when your husband prefers homemade lasagna to frozen pizza?

There are times when an assignment of priorities is both easy and helpful. But there are many other moments when the picture is not so clear, and the pieces keep shifting like the pattern in a kaleidoscope, which changes as you slowly rotate it in the light. There is no single clear priority all the time, or rigid, predetermined first-, second-, and third-place priority rankings which lead to the right choices.

What is this balancing act?

Another view of perspective for choice-making is the balancing act. Choices are made on the basis of how good we are at juggling.

Like a circus act, a mom takes one plate and spins it on a stick above her head. No problem. But then another plate is added, so she must spin both plates. A bit later, here comes another and then another until she is spinning four and then five plates above her head. As if this were not enough, some new responsibility hits her around one leg, and she finds she must stand with all her weight on only one foot. Looking down, she realizes that her once-secure footing has been replaced by a thin wire, suspended high above the ground. With perspiration beading her brow, she fights for balance while keeping all the plates in motion. Because, of course, she must.

Elizabeth Phillips Runkle shares her opinion on this balancing act from the view of a working woman. Responding to a Ph.D. on a television talk show, expounding on how to achieve total balance in her life and the world around her, Runkle writes,

> Balance? I could tell that woman on the TV a few things about balance.
>
> Balance is keeping the mom-mobile on the highway while simultaneously signing the homework paper that was due last week, tying the five-year-old's shoes, keeping him from hitting his sister, and getting the whole carload to school only

five minutes after the last bell and still arriving at work on time.

Balance is following the liturgy and looking prayerful while gently suspending the littlest one by the scruff of the neck and whispering in his ear, "We're in church! Cut out the anatomical sounds!"

Balance is holding a kid on each hip and a two-hundred-fifty pound dog on a leash while watching the clouds open up with a vengeance.

Balance is climbing to the mountaintop at work all day and digging through the mound of laundry at night.[4]

Life can't be kept neatly in balance. As soon as you decide that every child will only participate in one "outside" activity, your progeny are selected for children's chorale and make it to the finals of the state swim meet. We need something more than a balancing act to direct our perspective regarding choice-making.

SEASONED PERSPECTIVE

Perhaps the most sensible approach to understanding perspective for choice-making is the seasonal perspective. In this view, life is broken down into various seasons, each characterized by its own priorities and its own criteria for choice-making. Looking at the *whole* of life with all its seasons enables us to gain perspective within each season.

The Bible describes this seasonal perspective in the book of Ecclesiastes:

> There is a time for everything,
> and a season for every activity under heaven:
> a time to be born and a time to die,
> a time to plant and a time to uproot,
> a time to kill and a time to heal,
> a time to tear down and a time to build,
> a time to weep and a time to laugh,
> a time to mourn and a time to dance,

> a time to scatter stones and a time
> to gather them,
> a time to embrace and a time to refrain,
> a time to search and a time to give up,
> a time to keep and a time to throw away,
> a time to tear and a time to mend,
> a time to be silent and a time to speak,
> a time to love and a time to hate,
> a time for war and a time for peace (Eccl. 3:1–8).

A time to mother tiny children and a time to mother older ones. A time to hold babies and a time to let them go. A time to focus on our children and a time to give attention to ourselves and our dreams. As one mother of a preschooler put it:

> *I love autumn. It is my favorite time of year, but I felt frustrated that it is such a brief season until I realized that its beauty is so poignant because it is framed by summer and winter. As a mother of a preschooler, I have to remind myself that each stage of life has its immense wonder, yet they all must move on. It is only in the moving on that we can fully appreciate what has passed.*

In her book, *A Season at Home,* Debbie Barr writes about making choices with this seasonal perspective, which she describes as "sequencing," a process that allows women to concentrate on each of life's major tasks at the proper time.

Sequencing means narrowing the scope of our pursuits so as to give priority to children when they are young. Then, as the seasons of life unfold, we expand into other pursuits gradually, according to the guidance of God. Sequencing . . . allows us to say "I love you" to our children in the most convincing way possible: by being there during the season of their lives when they need the most nurture and physical care. As our children's seasons change, we move into new seasons as well.[5]

Such an understanding of the whole of life helps us to pay closer attention to where we are. We see the importance of choosing to invest in our children now—the season of their greatest need for us—knowing that other seasons will come later. "Not now, maybe later" points its finger, reminding us that we are not sacrificing ourselves forever. And reminding us that investment of time in our children now will pay dividends later as they become more independent, allowing us freedom to pursue other interests.

Mother-poet Joy Jacobs expresses her own commitment to sequencing in her "Mysteries of Motherhood":

> Yesterday I found a fingernail in the toaster,
> Today the dryer yields just seven socks.
> Ah, mysteries of life:
> Whence fingernails?
> Where socks?
> Where are the mates?
> And why not six or eight?
>
> I long to search for Holy Grails
> Or even joust at windmills. . . .
> Instead, I rewash glasses
> Left less than spot-free
> By eager childish hands
> And hang sheets out on windy days
> And never do catch sight
> of one brave armored knight.
>
> But when a little boy thanks God at night
> For "the best mommy in the world"—
> Strange windmills lose their charm
> And I'm content
> To fetch a grail of water
> Before he goes to sleep.
> Quixote, wait another year!
> I still am needed here.[6]

KEEPING THINGS IN PERSPECTIVE

Perspective is the ability to stand between yesterday and tomorrow and understand how today fits and what matters most. How very much moms of preschoolers need perspective! We need to know that we're making a difference when we put a bit of ourselves on the shelf for a while. We need to know that when we drop everything to hold our babies while they are sick, or disregard the clutter to read to our toddlers, or just be present as a "home base" from which our little ones can go out to explore—we need to know that we've chosen well.

Max Lucado captures our need for perspective as he writes about a group of climbers scaling a tall mountain while keeping their snow-capped goal in sight:

> On clear days the crested point reigned as king on the horizon. Its white tip jutted into the blue sky inviting admiration and offering inspiration.
>
> On days like this the hikers made the greatest progress. The peak stood above them like a compelling goal. Eyes were called upward. The walk was brisk. The cooperation was unselfish. . . .
>
> Yet on some days the peak of the mountain was hidden from view. The cloud covering would eclipse the crisp blueness with a drab, gray ceiling and block the vision of the mountaintop. On these days the climb became arduous. Eyes were downward and thoughts inward. The goal was forgotten. Tempers were short. Weariness was an uninvited companion. Complaints stung like thorns on the trail.
>
> We're like that, aren't we? As long as we can see our dream, as long as our goal is within eyesight, there is no mountain we can't climb or summit we can't scale. But take away our vision, block our view of the trail's end, and the result is as discouraging as the journey.[7]

Yes! In the daily grind of mothering little-bitty ones, moms need to remember the bigger picture. ❧

BUILDING BLOCKS

M **BUILDING BLOCK #1:**

Don't forget: Life can't be controlled.

Create your own Stress Sack with tangible reminders to let go of what's beyond your control. Here are some suggested items:

- *A Band-Aid®* to remind you that a hurting heart can be mended with God's healing love.
- *A tissue* to remind you to dry someone's tears with a kind word, a note, or a hug.
- *A piece of chalk* to use when something unpleasant happens, so you can "chalk it up" to experience.
- *An eraser* to remind you to wipe your slate clean of guilt and grudges every day.
- *A thumbtack* to remind you not to just sit on your problems. A-tack them one by one.
- *A favorite cartoon,* bumper sticker, or greeting card to remind you to laugh—often.
- *A small bottle* to remind you that God collects all your tears. He knows all about you (Ps. 56:8).
- *A small stone* to remind you God is your rock.
- *A nail* to remind you that Jesus coped with some pretty heavy stress, too.[8]

O **BUILDING BLOCK #2:**

Keep the "main thing" the main thing.

When you're perplexed and confused, read this piece of wise philosophy by Bob Benson:

Laughter in the Walls

I pass a lot of houses on my way home—
   some pretty,
   some expensive,
   some inviting—
but my heart always skips a beat
   when I turn down the road
and see my house nestled against the hill.
I guess I'm especially proud of the house and the way it
   looks because
I drew the plans myself.
It started out large enough for us—
   even had a study—
two teenaged boys now reside in there.
And it had a guest room—
   my girl and nine dolls are permanent guests.
   It had a small room Peg
had hoped would be her sewing room—
   two boys swinging on the dutch door
have claimed this room as their own.
So it really doesn't look right now
as if I'm much of an architect.
But it will get larger again—
one by one they will go away
   to work,
   to college,
   to service,
   to their own houses,
and then there will be room—
   a guest room,
   a study,
   and a sewing room
   for just the two of us.
   But it won't be empty—
   every corner,
   every nick
   in the coffee table

will be crowded with memories.
Memories of picnics,
parties, Christmases, bedside vigils, summers,
fires, winters, going barefoot, leaving for vacation, cats,
conversations, black eyes,
graduations, first dates,
ball games, arguments,
washing dishes, bicycles,
dogs, boat rides,
getting home from vacation,
meals, rabbits and
a thousand other things
that fill the lives
of those who would raise five.
And Peg and I will sit
quietly by the fire
and listen to the
laughter in the walls.[9]

BUILDING BLOCK #3:

Make the most of life's irretrievable moments.

Every day is priceless and will never return. Decide now that you won't waste a single one.

A New Day

This is the beginning of a new day. God has given me this day to use as I will. I can waste it—or use it for good, but what I do today is important, because I am exchanging a day of my life for it! When tomorrow comes, this day will be gone forever, leaving in its place something that I have traded for it. I want it to be gain, and not loss; good, and not evil; success, and not failure; in order that I shall not regret the price that I have paid for it.[10]

BUILDING BLOCK #4:

Keep a fresh perspective.

Here's an idea to help you appreciate your children, right where they are. Copy this poem on a piece of paper and put it on your refrigerator, along with your child's handprint:

> Sometimes you get discouraged
> Because I am so small
> And always leave my fingerprints
> On furniture and walls.
> But every day I'm growing up
> And soon I'll be so tall,
> That all those little handprints
> Will be hard to recall.
> So here's a special handprint
> Just so that you can say
> This is how my fingers looked
> When I placed them here today.
>
> —Anonymous

BUILDING BLOCK #5:

Root out myth from reality.

Determine some of your own mothering myths and realities by answering these questions:

1. What are some of the "ditties" about mothering that echo in your mind like a broken record? (Example: "If it's worth doing, it's worth doing well.") Which ones are valuable to keep? Which are not?
2. What are your greatest fears or worries as a mother?
3. What are your greatest frustrations?
4. Which answers from the last two questions can you control?

5. Which are beyond your control?
6. How will you intentionally "let go" of what you can't control?
7. What do you want most for your child? Are your goals apparent?
8. What are you doing to make progress towards these goals?
9. What are your priorities in this season of life?
10. How are they different from your life priorities before you had children?
11. What different priorities will you have when all your kids are in school? When all of them have left home?
12. What do you like best about this season of life?
13. What advice about this season would you offer to a new mother?
14. How do you follow that advice?

BUILDING BLOCK #6:

Finding perspective takes time.

Finding what matters most in life sometimes means taking a break, wasting time, or doing nothing, as this piece describes:

I wasted an hour one morning beside a mountain stream,
I seized a cloud from the sky above, and fashioned
   myself a dream;
In the hush of the early twilight, far from the haunts of men,
I wasted a summer evening, and fashioned my dream again.
Wasted? Perhaps.
Folks say so who never have walked with God,
When lanes are purple with lilacs or yellow with goldenrod.
But I have found strength of my labors in that one short
   evening hour,
I have found joy and contentment; I have found peace and
   power.

My dreaming has left me a treasure, a hope that is strong and
  true,
From wasted hours I have built my life, and found my
  faith anew.

—Anonymous

BUILDING BLOCK #7:

Trust God.

Remember this promise: "For I know the plans I have for
you, declares the LORD, plans to prosper you and not to harm
you, plans to give you hope and a future" (Jer. 29:11).

FOR FURTHER READING:

Gift from the Sea, Anne Morrow Lindbergh
The Joy of Being a Woman, Ingrid Trobisch
Ordering Your Private World, Gordon MacDonald
A Season at Home, Debbie Barr
Seven Habits of Highly Effective People, Steven Covey
What Is a Family?, Edith Schaeffer
When You Feel Like Screaming, Pat Holt and Grace Ketterman

Mothering Maxim

— ❧ —

Fit today into the
BIGGER PICTURE
of life.

Nine

Hope:

Sometimes I wonder if there is more to life

S he threw back the sliding door. It banged against its casing, rattling the glass. Thick, humid air wet her face. She didn't care. She stepped outside and slid the door shut behind her. No good. Here came Samuel and Elizabeth to the door, smashing their faces up against the glass, their hot breath creating circles of steam on its surface. "*Mommy!* Come back in here right now!" Samuel hollered. Elizabeth raised her blanket, her face puckering in whimpers.

Carla opened the door a few inches, reached in her hand, and yanked the drape pull. The drapes jerked and bumped across the opening. She shut the door again, held it closed, and sank down with her back against it, hugging her knees.

Now they came at her from beneath the curtains, pushing the drapes up in uneven lumps with their heads, their hair staticky and clinging to the fabric. "MOMMY!"

"Samuel and Elizabeth . . . LEAVE ME ALONE!" Carla screamed. Both children stared wide-eyed at their usually composed mother. Elizabeth's whimpers turned to wails. Samuel looked pious and put a protective arm about his baby sister as he led her out from underneath the drapes.

Carla let out a long and loud sigh. She stared back at her own reflection from the flat surface of the patio door. Creases in her brow. Bags under her eyes. Hair slicked back in a quick ponytail. Sweats that couldn't hide the presence of fifteen stubborn, ever-present pounds. Just like her kids—always there even when she didn't want them to be.

She turned from the reflection and sat down on the top step, her back against the door. She looked out at the small yard littered with big wheels and sandbox toys. The kids had been digging where the patch of lawn was giving way to dirt. She didn't care. The "patio" was just a gray concrete slab, twelve feet by fifteen feet. Cracks ran from under her feet out to the edge of the "lawn." Raising her eyes to the sky, she saw more gray. Gray, gray, gray. Sky. Patio. Her mood.

It was only three o'clock in the afternoon, but she'd been up since five A.M. She'd already been to the store and the park. She'd made lunch. Then she'd read to the kids and put them down for naps. But they wouldn't sleep. She'd finally given up and just sat in front of *Oprah,* hoping for a bit of release. That's when they'd come at her with puzzles, books, and then whines to put a movie in the VCR. It was too much.

"I can't do this," Carla spat out the words. *I'm tired. I'm angry. I've got nothing left,* she thought to herself. *I didn't think mothering would be like this! I thought I'd rock my babies in snuggly blankets. That they'd always smell good and smile at me. That they'd sleep at some point during their lifetimes—and that I could do some things I wanted to do. I never dreamed I'd be losing it like this with my kids, wanting them to just leave me alone.*

Her silent monologue ceased. She simply sat, staring blankly ahead.

And then she felt a *clunk* against her back through the glass. Samuel was hurling Legos® at the curtains, trying to get her attention. Carla's chest tightened. Her head pounded. *I really can't do this,* she repeated to herself. *I can't go back in there.* Lifting her eyes heavenward, she asked aloud, "Is there any hope for me?"

HOPELESS SITUATIONS

Have you ever felt like this mother? Your husband just lost his job, and you're not sure how you'll pay the bills. Your mother has cancer and needs you, but you have three little ones who also need you. You're pregnant again and wonder in your heart if you can really afford . . . love . . . or cope with another child. Your marriage is stale and old. Your best friend is moving away, far away, and you wonder how you'll make it without her. Your neighborhood is full of crime—it's not safe to walk to the store anymore. Your house is a mess. Not only is there junk everywhere, but the paint is peeling, the bathtub drain is clogged, and the carpet is covered with stains. Your children aren't what you had in mind. One has been diagnosed with a disorder you don't understand, and the other seems uncontrollable.

You feel like you can't do it anymore. It's too much. Life isn't turning out the way you expected, and there's not enough of you left to handle it.

MISPLACED HOPE

You look for hope anywhere you think you might find it. If you could only change your circumstances, even for just a little while. . . . *A vacation! That's what I need!* you think. So you make a plan, pack up husband and kids and a two bags full of toys to keep them entertained in a cramped car, drive all night and half the next day, and check into a hotel exhausted. The room doesn't have that lovely mountain view promised in the brochure. It looks out over the parking lot. The kids are raring to go, and you want to sleep. It rains for three days. Your youngest gets sick. And the sun comes out the day you leave.

Then you try optimism. You read an article in a magazine about how positive thinking can help you to be happier and healthier. The pessimist's feelings of helplessness and hopelessness damage the body's natural immune system, so the writer says. On the other hand, optimism protects one against illness. You wake in the morning, telling yourself you'll look on the bright side, but by nine o'clock you've been forced to deal with the dog mess on the carpet, spoiled milk in the refrigerator, and a dead battery in your car. *What* bright side?

Ah. People. Surely you can count on another person to give you hope—maybe your husband. Between errands and during precious naptime, you squeeze in a trial run on a new recipe, set a romantic table, and put the kids to bed early so you can be alone with him. But he wants to watch the game on TV. Or, you call up your best friend, arrange for a baby-sitter, and set a date for lunch—out. But she gets the flu. And you end up taking her kids as well as yours so she can sleep.

Okay. One last try. You get spiritual. You hear on a talk show that if you look for the goodness inside yourself, you'll find the confidence and comfort and strength your heart desires. So you look down. But all you see is one mistake after another. Inadequacies. Failures. Fears. Insecurities. *What* goodness?

This is the worst yet. There's no way to take care of this feeling of emptiness and no option left to cover it up. You suddenly know you have nothing left. You can't do this for yourself, and you wonder if there is any reason left to hope.

HIGH HOPES

This is the toughest stuff of life. It's the place we all come to eventually. It hurts. It's called "reaching the end of ourselves."

But there is Someone who understands. He knows that what you want and need won't be found in a vacation, in positive thinking, in people, or in an attempt to reach down within yourself. He knows that you can't give yourself what you need. He knows you're tired. He knows you're empty. He knows there's nothing left.

How does he know? He knows because he is God. And he understands because he himself lived what you are living. He sent his Son Jesus to walk the earth. He ate and slept . . . and *didn't* sleep. He endured poverty, sickness, rejection, beatings, misjudgment, and exhaustion. He knows your struggles.

And he wants to help you by bringing you into a relationship with him. You see, hope comes in a relationship. It is through a relationship with Jesus that your needs can be met completely and permanently.

Remember when you looked down into your heart to find the "goodness" within you and, instead, you found all those bad places? That's because while there are definitely good aspects to each of us, all of us fall short of perfection. We sometimes yell at our children. We're selfish with our time. We argue with our husbands. We're jealous of our neighbors. We hold grudges, lose our patience, and sometimes even hate a few people.

There's a word for this condition. The Bible calls it *sin*. Sin separates us from God because he is holy and perfect and can't dwell in the presence of sin. But where does that leave us? We're separated from the very Source that can provide help for us.

Good news! God loves you. And he chose to take care of this sin problem himself by allowing his Son, Jesus, to die on the cross. His death pays for your sins and makes it possible for you to be forgiven for all the sinful spots—once and for all. Even when you don't deserve it. That's called *grace*. You've heard the old hymn, "Amazing Grace." Well, God's forgiveness *is* amazing. We don't deserve it. But we have it if we want it.

Do you want it? Do you want to know God's love?

You may still have questions. That's okay. There are numbers of people who can help you find answers—counselors, pastors or ministers, friends. There are books you can read that will help you make sense of this personal relationship with Jesus. Check the recommended reading list in the Building Blocks section at the end of this chapter. Or pick up the Bible and simply start reading, say, in the gospel of John or Mark, and you'll find out lots more about Jesus.

You probably won't understand it all. Don't worry. You don't have to. You don't have to understand electricity to use it, do you? You just have to plug something in or turn on a switch. A relationship with Jesus begins when you give what you know about yourself and your needs to what you know about him.

So how do you begin this relationship that provides you with the hope your heart desires? That's easy. Just ask. Remember that emptiness inside you? That's the path that leads you to Jesus. As long as you believe you can take care of everything yourself and that you have all the goodness inside you to meet all your needs, you won't be able to receive the help Jesus has to offer. But when you figure out that you can't meet all your needs, that there is a big empty hole in your heart that nothing else seems to fill—then you can turn to Jesus and ask for help.

It's like this. A little boy was struggling to move a wagon, loaded with his prized possessions. His father watched his struggle from the front porch.

Sweating and puffing, the boy hollered at his dad, "I can't budge this thing!"

"Have you tried everything you can try?"

"Yes!" sighed the tired boy.

"No, you haven't," called the father. "You haven't asked me for help."

In the gospel of Matthew, Jesus speaks comforting words to every mother of preschoolers: "Come to me, all you who are weary and burdened, and I will give you rest" (Matt. 11:28). It is to you that Jesus speaks these words. You can begin a relationship of hope with him. All you have to do is ask.

Pray this simple prayer:

Dear Jesus, I'm empty. When I look inside myself, I see the soiled places that I now know are sin. Because of that sin, I know I cannot have a relationship with you. I need your help. I believe that you died on the cross for me and for my sins. Please forgive me for my sins. I want to trust you as my Savior, and I want to know you as my Lord. Please come into my life and begin a relationship with me. Amen.

If you prayed that prayer just now as you read it, you can be sure that today you have a new reason to hope! You may not feel so different immediately, but you can start living with the promise that Jesus loves you and that he will help you on a day-to-day basis. You no longer have to live this life alone or dependent only upon yourself and your abilities. In fact, life was designed to be lived in partnership with Jesus, leaning on him through everything that comes, drawing from his strength, depending upon his wisdom.

HOPE FOR ALL OUR NEEDS

When we look back through this book, chapter by chapter, and revisit each need in the light of a relationship with Jesus, we can see that he can be like sunbeams shining through the clouds on a gray day. Let's look at some of the things we've learned, one by one.

Significance: Sometimes I wonder if mothering matters.

It does. We spent twenty-something pages explaining why it matters. Add to the truth of this chapter that all our "doing" will never be enough to earn us the kind of consistent significance in life that we long for; that God alone provides the ultimate meaning for our lives. Suddenly, our doing doesn't define us or confine us! All at once we're free to be the best mothers we can be because our ultimate worth is not dependent upon our role of mothering.

Identity: Sometimes I'm not sure who I am.

God made us. Each one of us. And we are precious in his sight. When we learn to see ourselves as God sees us—forgiven and free from sin—we are truly free to drop our burdens of guilt over not being good enough, and become all he created us to be.

Growth: Sometimes I long to develop who I am.

God has placed unique potential within each of us. And that potential can be fully developed and completely fulfilled only through a relationship with him. We find that change and growth are possible as he changes us.

Intimacy: Sometimes I long to be understood.

As much as we'd like to, we can't always count on other people. Eventually, they will disappoint us. Nobody's perfect. They'll hurt our feelings or let us down. Only God is perfect. And only his love for us is pure and unconditional. In a relationship with Jesus, we can find the intimacy and understanding we need. He knows us the best and loves us the most.

Instruction: Sometimes I don't know what to do.

In the Bible we will find many practical principles and truths that tell us how to live. There is also truth in the world that can provide us with direction, because all real truth is God's truth. This truth helps us make good choices.

Help: Sometimes I need to share the load.

We weren't meant to mother alone. When we admit our need for help, God can meet it. He wants us to learn to trust him to be in control of the uncontrollable part of our lives.

Recreation: Sometimes I need a break.

Recreation is really re-creation. God created us with the need to rest. He also makes us new creatures when we come into a relationship with Jesus. Each day is a new beginning when we begin it with him. And he refreshes and renews us on an ongoing basis as we seek him.

Perspective: Sometimes I lose my focus.

Perspective means developing a God-view of life. When we learn to see life as he does, to value what he values, to evaluate decisions and daily matters in terms of what matters in eternity, we obtain a whole new perspective.

Real hope is finding the Source that meets all needs.

A RELATIONSHIP OF HOPE

Beginning a relationship with Jesus will not mean that all your problems will fade away. You won't find yourself suddenly perfect in all your interactions. Nope. Beginning a relationship with Jesus is just that: *a beginning*. It will take time for him to change you. You will gradually learn to trust him with more and more areas of your world as you get to know him better.

As in all relationships, your relationship with Jesus will grow and develop as you work at it. As you invest yourself, you'll reap dividends. As you learn, you'll grow. Remember, this relationship with Jesus allows you to have a relationship with the God of the universe! Because Jesus died for our sins and God raised him from the dead, Jesus is alive and stands ready to be active in your life!

I see now that my real need has always been for God. Motherhood is too hard to go it alone. I was so overwhelmed with the birth of my second son that I didn't think I'd make it. I remember sitting on the stairs of our townhouse, holding my baby while the toddler was "somewhere," and I cried out that I just couldn't do it anymore. Shortly after that, I accepted Christ. Now he does it and I help.

Two practices will be vital to growing in your relationship with Jesus.

Talking

As in all relationships, communication is essential to knowing. In order to get to know God better, we have to talk to him.

Talking with God doesn't have to be complicated or even very formal. Prayer is merely having a conversation with God. It's talking to him and telling him what's on your mind and in your heart. In his book, *Prayer,* Richard Foster describes how to talk to God: "Simple Prayer involves ordinary people bringing ordinary concerns to a loving and compassionate Father."[1] And prayer is regular. Foster offers a sample of this kind of regular talking to God: "Sometimes Simple Prayer is called the 'Prayer of Beginning Again,'" Foster writes. "We make mistakes, we sin, we fall down, but each time we get up and begin again. We pray again. We seek to follow God again. And again we are defeated. Never mind. We confess and begin again . . . and again . . . and again."[2]

Set aside a time to talk to God each day. Maybe when you first open your eyes in the morning before you even throw back the covers. Maybe as you rock your little ones to sleep at naptime or bedtime. Maybe the first few minutes of their naptime. But keep looking until you find a regular time to meet with God.

Besides getting into a routine of prayer, try talking to him in the day-to-day business of your life. As you wash the dishes, take out the trash, drive to the store. God is always present and available. We don't have to make an appointment to get his attention. When you're wondering how to handle your child's tantrum, ask Jesus. If you're not sure if you should be working or not during these years, talk it over with him. You don't have to keep all your questions inside. When you're in a relationship with Jesus, he is ready and willing to hear and help.

Listening

As important as it is to talk to God, it is equally vital to listen to what he says. No, he doesn't usually communicate with folks through an audible voice. But he does get his thoughts across through his Holy Spirit. Sometimes he'll speak to you when you're reading the Bible (his Word). And sometimes he'll speak through relationships with other people who know him (Christians).

When you pray, pause long enough to "listen." God may want to tell you something in response to your prayer. Sometimes we simply don't have what we need because we're never still enough to listen to what God is trying to get across to us. But as we practice listening, we'll learn how to hear his whispers more and more often.

Find a translation of the Bible that is easy to read and understand. The *New International Version* is a good one. Some paraphrases are also helpful as we first begin to read God's Word—Eugene Peterson's *The Message,* for example. Start out with the psalms or a Gospel (Matthew, Mark, Luke, or John) or a small New Testament book, like Galatians or Ephesians, and go on from there. Because the Bible is God's Word, it is the major tool available to us for getting to know him. Don't neglect it.

We can also listen to others who know God. When we share our concerns and questions with those who have been in a relationship with God longer, we find strength and help. God will use his people to help you. And before you know it, he'll use you to help others! This is what the church is all about. Visit a church in your area. Find out about their beliefs and whether or not they match up with what you read in the Bible. Attend services and consider becoming a member.

But you will soon learn that "church" means much more than a building. God intended his people to be in fellowship together, to study the Bible together, to worship together, to learn to depend upon each other, and to reach out to others— together. This is called "community" and within this kind of loving and sharing atmosphere, many of us find the sense of family we might not have had in our own nuclear families. In community, we focus and grow in our relationships with God and with other people. The Bible teaches us that we must be in intentional Christian community in order to become the people God intends us to be. So find a church home. Join a Bible study—a group of folks who come together to study God's Word. Get involved in serving others and meeting their needs. Share with your husband and your children what you are learning about Jesus.

Your relationship with God is a relationship between living souls. It will grow and change and deepen as you invest yourself in it. You can expect to change and for your relationships with others to be different as well. Jesus loves us too much to leave us just the way we are. You may discover that you will have to apologize after making a mistake rather than ignoring your offense. You may find that you need to grow in an area of patience or humility. You might even find that you have whole areas of your life that Jesus wants to touch and heal. He may want you to risk—to venture out into something you've never done before, to a place where you've never been. But even the desire for these changes comes from God. And he will help us through them. That's one of his promises.

Is there hope for you? You bet. Trust him. Jesus knows what you need. And he can meet those needs better than you can meet them alone.

In the book of Isaiah, the prophet describes God's tender care for his nation of Israel. Using a shepherd metaphor, he encourages his people. God's words in this Old Testament book—written some four thousand years ago—are for every mother of preschoolers today: "He tends his flock like a shepherd: He gathers the lambs in his arms and carries them close to his heart; he gently leads those that have young" (Isa. 40:11). ॐ

BUILDING BLOCKS

BUILDING BLOCK #1:

Words for inspiration and understanding.

Here are some quotes about our need for God and a relationship with him through his Son, Jesus:

> You have made us for yourself, O God, and our hearts are restless till they find rest in you.—Augustine's *Confessions*

> Man searches in vain, but finds nothing to help him, other than to see an infinite emptiness that can only be filled by One who is infinite and unchanging. In other words, it can only be filled by God Himself.—Blaise Pascal

> The soul hardly ever realizes it, but whether he is a believer or not, his loneliness is really a homesickness for God. —Hubert Van Zeller, *We Die Standing Up*

> Our problem is not so much that God doesn't give us what we hope for as it is that we don't know the right thing for which to hope.... Hope is not what you expect.—Max Lucado, *God Came Near*

> After I became a parent, it was easier for me to grasp the concept of God's love. As I went through all the triumphs

and traumas of parenting and found myself still constantly loving my son, only then did I begin to understand God's ability to love *me* unconditionally.[3]

BUILDING BLOCK #2:

Begin a relationship with Jesus.

Many people seek to fill that God–shaped emptiness with pleasure, prosperity, or power—anything but God, and yet the emptiness remains. Why? Because finite things can never fill an infinite emptiness. The search for fulfillment in life must begin with God.

Did you know that there is a God who is looking for you?

God's Position

1. The God who searches is a God of love. His desire is to have a loving relationship with us.

For God so loved the world, that he gave his one and only Son, that whoever believes in him shall not perish but have eternal life.—John 3:16

2. However, the God who searches is also a God of perfection. His absolute moral perfection is the standard upon which the relationship is based.

Be perfect, therefore, as your heavenly Father is perfect. —Matt. 5:48

Our Condition

People who are searching for God must realize three things:

1. They fall short of God's standard of perfection.

For all have sinned and fall short of the glory of God. —Rom. 3:23

2. They face God's penalty of eternal separation.

For the wages of sin is death [eternal separation], but the gift of God is eternal life in Christ Jesus our Lord.—Rom. 6:23

3. They fail to enjoy God's love.

But your iniquities have separated you from your God; your sins have hidden his face from you, so that he will not hear.—Isa. 59:2

God's Provision

God, in the person of Jesus Christ, took the initiative in searching for us.

1. God substituted Christ's perfection for our imperfection through his death, burial, and resurrection.

For Christ died for sins once for all, the righteous for the unrighteous, to bring you to God. He was put to death in the body but made alive by the Spirit.—1 Peter 3:18.

2. Through Jesus, God satisfied both his love and perfection, thereby making a relationship with him possible.

This is love: not that we loved God, but that he loved us and sent his Son as an atoning sacrifice [satisfactory payment] for our sins.—1 John 4:10

Our Decision

The search for God ends in a choice: To accept or reject Christ's perfect payment for your sins.

1. Accepting God's gift involves admitting the truth about yourself—that you have failed to measure up to God's standards and are separated from him.

For the wages of sin is death [eternal separation], but the gift of God is eternal life in Christ Jesus our Lord.—Rom. 6:23

2. Accepting God's gift involves transferring your trust from yourself to Jesus Christ.

Yet to all who received him, to those who believed in his name, he gave the right to become children of God. —John 1:12

Now you can have a personal relationship with God.[4]

BUILDING BLOCK #3:

Build a hope chest for hearts in need.
Always Deeper Still

By Gary Driscoll and Marty Hennis.
©1990 by Word Music (a division of Word Inc.) and
These Three Music. All rights reserved. Used by permission.

I've been right where you are
That place where faith becomes so hard
  and you find yourself wond'rin'
  just where life went wrong
  Your dearest dreams have died
And left the biggest emptiness inside
Now your heart is askin' how it can go on
  Well it may seem like God's unaware
But take it from someone who's been there
No one falls beneath the Father's reach
  to rescue his children

Even when you sink down
  to the bottom of the well
And knowin' when hope will come
  is awfully hard to tell
  no matter how hurt you are
  no matter how badly you've been scared
Even when the climbin' looks so steep
And you think that you've fallen in too deep
  know that God's love is runnin'
always deeper still
Know that God's love is runnin'
  always deeper still
  I felt like a castaway
  Stranded and so far away
Unsure if God could hear me callin'
  His name

The days seemed to last so long
   Without an answer to lean on
I wondered if the waiting would all be
     in vain
   But just when hope became
   so tangled and tossed
That I'd almost given myself up for lost
That's when the Father proved to me
   His love never ever fails

Because He Lives

Words by William J. & Gloria Gaither.
Music by William J. Gaither. Copyright 1971 by William J. Gaither.
All rights reserved. Used by permission.

God sent His Son, they called Him Jesus,
He came to love, heal, and forgive;
He lived and died to buy my pardon,
An empty grave is there to prove my Savior lives.

Because He lives I can face tomorrow,
Because He lives all fear is gone;
Because I know He holds the future.
And life is worth the living just because He lives.

How sweet to hold a newborn baby,
And feel the pride and joy He gives;
But greater still the calm assurance,
This child can face uncertain days because He lives.

And then one day I'll cross the river,
I'll fight life's final war with pain;
And then as death gives way to victory,
I'll see the lights of glory and I'll know He lives.

From the Bible:

Hope deferred makes the heart sick, but a longing fulfilled is a tree of life.—Prov. 13:12

Now faith is being sure of what we hope for and certain of what we do not see.—Heb. 11:1

And my God will meet all your needs according to his glorious riches in Christ Jesus.—Phil. 4:19

For I am convinced that neither death nor life, neither angels nor demons, neither the present nor the future, nor any powers, neither height nor depth, nor anything else in all creation, will be able to separate us from the love of God that is in Christ Jesus our Lord.—Rom. 8:38–39

BUILDING BLOCK #5:

Tear down the stumbling blocks to faith.

Many times we run into obstacles or barriers that keep us from embracing faith in God.

The Emotional Barrier—A set of negative feelings based on bad experiences with believers or with organized religion. We are confronted by the emotional barrier when we reject Christ because we have felt put down or pressured. It may seem that all believers in Christ are pushy and hypocritical.

The Intellectual Barrier—A tendency to disregard or reject Christ based upon bad information or misconceptions. We face an intellectual barrier, for instance, when we reject Christ because we assume the Bible is full of mistakes, or because we just cannot understand how a loving God could allow suffering in the world.

The Volitional Barrier—A natural inclination to resist examining spiritual things, or to reject Christ outright based upon independence, pride, or stubbornness. The Bible says this independence is rooted in our sinful nature. We encounter a volitional barrier when we refuse to examine the evidence for Christianity because we are afraid of what we might have to give up. Another friend may evidence the volitional barrier when she sees the truth of Christianity but simply won't take the next step and receive Christ.[5]

BUILDING BLOCK #6:

Learn about faith.

Faith is . . .

. . . not a leap in the dark nor a mystical experience nor an indefinable encounter with someone—but trust in One who has explained himself in a Person—Christ, in an historical record—the Bible . . . remembering that in the kingdom of God everything is based on promise not on feeling.

. . . confidence in God's faithfulness to me in an uncertain world, on an uncharted course, through an unknown future.

. . . reliance on the certainty that God has a pattern for my life when everything seems meaningless.

. . . thanking God for his gift of emotional health, not assuming it all stems from my ability to cope with life.

. . . not a vague hope of a happy hereafter, but an assurance of heaven based on my trust in Christ's death as payment for my sins.

. . . refusing to feel guilty over *past* confessed sins, when God, the Judge, has sovereignly declared me—"PARDONED!"

. . . realizing that God is the God of *now*, carrying on his purposes in every tedious, dull, stupid, boring, empty minute of my life.

. . . ceasing to worry, leaving the *future* to the God who controls the future.[5]

FOR FURTHER READING:

For Questions About Faith or Jesus

Answers to Tough Questions, Josh McDowell and Don Stewart
I'm Glad You Asked, Ken Boa & Larry Moody
More Than a Carpenter, Josh McDowell

For Developing a Relationship with Jesus

Beyond Ourselves, Catherine Marshall
Experiencing God, Henry T. Blackaby and Claude V. King
Eerdman's Book of Famous Prayers, compiled by Veronica Zundel
Honest to God, Bill Hybels
Mere Christianity, C. S. Lewis
The Mother's Devotional Bible (New International Version), March '97
  release
No Wonder They Call Him Savior, Max Lucado
My Heart, Christ's Home, Robert Munger
Practicing the Presence of God, Brother Lawrence
Pursuit of God, A. W. Tozer
Through Gates of Splendor, Elisabeth Elliot

Mothering Maxim

— ❧ —

Hope is a personal
relationship with God,
who meets all our needs.

The MOPS Story

It was a Tuesday morning, at about 9:30. They had each faced spilled cereal, tangled hair, and a few had even been forced to change their outfits due to last-minute baby throw-up on a shoulder or lap. They had driven, or pushed strollers, to the church and had dropped their little ones off in the nursery. They had made it!

And now they sat, knees almost touching, in the circle of children's chairs from the Sunday school room. Hands held cups of hot coffee and doughnuts in utter freedom because this treat did not have to be shared with a child's sticky fingers. Mouths moved in eager, uninterrupted conversation. Eyes sparkled with enthusiasm. Hearts stirred with understanding. Needs were met.

That morning, back in 1973, was the first morning of MOPS. From its humble beginnings in a church in Wheat Ridge, Colorado, with only a handful of moms, MOPS International now charters MOPS groups in almost one thousand churches in all fifty of the United States and in twelve other countries.

Some forty thousand moms are touched by the local MOPS group and many, many more are encouraged through the media arms of MOPS: *Mom Sense* radio and newsletter and publications such as this book. Mission MOPS is available as well, offering the support of MOPS to moms in areas where special assistance is needed and providing a sistering network between suburbia and cities.

MOPS grew out of a desire to meet the nine needs of every mother of preschoolers. Today, when a mom enters a MOPS meeting, she is greeted by a friendly face and escorted to the

MOPPETS program where she leaves her children for the two and a half hours of the MOPS day. In MOPPETS, children from infancy through kindergarten experience a safe and caring environment while being introduced to crafts, songs, and learning opportunities. For many families, this is the first or only opportunity for children to enjoy making new friends and learning about God.

Once her children are settled, the MOPS mom joins a program tailor-made to meet her needs. She can grab something good to eat and not have to share it! She can finish a sentence and not have to speak in Children-ese!

The program begins with a brief lesson taught by a Titus Woman (an older mom who's been through the challenging early years of mothering and who can share from her experience and from the truths taught in the Bible). Then the women move into small discussion groups where there are no "wrong answers" and each mom is free to share her joys and struggles with other moms who truly understand her feelings. In these moments, long-lasting friendships are often made on the common ground of finally being understood.

From here, the women participate in a craft activity. For moms who are often frustrated by the impossibility of completing anything in their unpredictable days, this activity is deeply satisfying. It provides a sense of accomplishment and growth for many moms.

Because moms of preschoolers themselves lead MOPS, the program also offers women a chance to develop their leadership skills and other latent talents. It takes organization, up-front abilities, financial management, creativity, and management skills to run a MOPS program successfully.

By the time they finish the MOPS meeting and pick up their children, the moms feel refreshed and better able to mother. MOPS helps them recognize that moms have needs too! And when they take the time to meet those needs, they find they are more effective in meeting the needs of their families. This is how one mom described MOPS:

MOPS means I am able to share the joys, frustrations and insecurities of being a mom. Our meetings provide the opportunity to hear someone else say, "I was up all night," or "They're driving me crazy!" or "He doesn't understand." While listening to others, I may discover a fresh idea or a new perspective that helps me tackle the job of parenting, home management, or being a good wife. It's important to feel normal and not alone. Burdens are lifted when the woman next to me says, "I know exactly how you feel." MOPS is a place for my children to interact with peers while I savor some uninterrupted conversation.

I was not a Christian when I began attending MOPS. Over the past year I have experienced tremendous spiritual growth and I know that MOPS was a contributor to that growth. Now, fellowship with other Christian women is an integral reason for me to attend. I thank the Lord for bringing me and my children to MOPS.

The MOPS program also enables moms to reach out and help other moms, fulfilling not only a need to belong and be understood but a need to help others. Here are two examples:

MOPS helped me when I was six months pregnant, the mother of a four-year-old, new to the area with no family, no doctors, no baby-sitters, no friends.

I attended a MOPS group only two times before my baby was hospitalized with a critical illness. Women from this MOPS group provided meals, cleaned my house, even employed my teenage daughter as a baby-sitter to keep her occupied while my baby was hospitalized for fifty days. I felt overwhelmed by this kind of outreach from moms who hardly knew me. My baby is recovering, and I will forever be changed myself. ❧

MOPS International
1311 S. Clarkson St.
Denver, CO 80210

Growing Together

Once upon a time there was a little grape stem.
She was so glad to be alive. She drank water and
minerals from the soil and grew and grew. She was
young and strong and could manage quite well . . .
All By Herself.
But the wind was cruel, the rain was harsh, and the snow
was not one bit understanding. The little grape stem
experienced pain. She drooped, weak and suffering.
"It would be so easy to stop trying to grow, to stop trying
to live," thought the little stem. She felt poorly. The winter
was long, and she was weary. But then the little stem
heard a voice. It was another grape stem calling out to her . . .
"Here, reach out, hang on to me." But the little stem hesitated.
What would this mean? she wondered. For you see, the little
stem had always managed quite well . . .
All By Herself.
Then ever so cautiously, she reached out toward the other
grape stem. "See, I can help you," it said. "Just wind your
tendrils about me, and I will help you lift your head."
And the little stem trusted. Suddenly, she could stand
straight again. The wind came . . . and the rain . . . and the snow.
But when it came, the little stem was clinging to many other
stems. And although the stems were swayed by the wind . . .
and frozen by the snow, they stood strongly united to each other.
And in their quiet strength, they could smile and grow.
One day, the little stem said, "Here, hang on . . . I will help you."
And another stem reached up to the little grape stem.
And together, all the stems grew.
Leaves budded . . . flowers bloomed . . . and finally
the grapes formed.
And the grapes fed many.

—Anonymous

To find out if there is a MOPS group near you, or if you're interested in finding out how to start a MOPS group in your community, please write or call the MOPS International office:

MOPS International
1311 S. Clarkson St.
Denver, CO 80210
Phone: (303) 733-5353
Fax: (303) 733-5770

Introduction

1. Dr. Lawrence J. Crabb, *Basic Principles of Biblical Counseling* (Grand Rapids, MI: Zondervan, 1975), 53.

Chapter One

Significance: Sometimes I wonder if mothering matters

1. Phyllis Diller in *A Mother Is to Cherish* (Nashville, TN: Thomas Nelson, 1994).

2. Anne Morrow Lindbergh, *Gift from the Sea* (New York: Pantheon, 1955), 46–47.

3. Joan France, "A 'Caretaker' Generation," *Newsweek* (January 29, 1990): 16.

4. Jill Zook-Jones interview with Brenda Hunter, "The Maternal Imperative," *Christianity Today* (March 7, 1994): 15.

5. *Starting Points: The Report on the Carnegie Task Force on Meeting the Needs of Young Children* (New York: Carnegie Corporation of New York, April 1994).

6. Sandra Pipp in Mary McArthur, "Whose Baby Are You?" *Colorado Alumnus* (December 1993): 5.

7. Sigmund Freud, *Outline of Psychoanalysis SE 23* (London: Hogarth Press, 1940), 188.

8. Dr. Marianne Neifert in Betty Johnson, "The Juggling Act of Dr. Mom," *Virtue* (March/April 1994): 38.

9. Jan Johnson, "Stay at Home Moms," *Virtue* (January/February, 1990): 32.

10. Juanita Fletcher, "Rostrum," *U.S. News and World Report* (August 8, 1988): 8.

11. Quoted in Bob Kelly's *Reflections* (1990).

Chapter Two

Identity: Sometimes I'm not sure who I am

1. Gregg Lewis, "Good News About Me," *Campus Life* (October 1986): 31.

2. Erik Fromm, *The Art of Living* (New York: Harper & Row, 1956), 43.

3. B. J. Cohler and H. V. Grunebaum, *Mothers, Grandmothers, and Daughters* (New York: Wiley, 1981) in Brenda Hunter, *Home by Choice* (Portland, OR: Multnomah Press, 1993), 32.

4. John Trent, *Life Mapping* (Colorado Springs, CO: Focus on the Family, 1994), 81.

5. Martha Thatcher, "The Most Difficult Love," *Discipleship Journal 35* (1986): 19.

6. Cecil Osborne, *The Art of Learning to Love Yourself* (Grand Rapids, MI: Zondervan, 1976), 38.

7. Valerie Bell, *Getting Out of Your Kids' Faces and Into Their Hearts* (Grand Rapids, MI: Zondervan, 1994), 73.

8. Ibid.

9. A. W. Tozer, *That Incredible Christian* (Harrisburg, PA: Christian Publications, 1964), 102–3. Used by permission.

10. Reprinted from Gary Smalley and John Trent, Ph.D., *Two Sides of Love,* Copyright 1990, Gary Smalley and John Trent, Ph.D. Used by permission of Focus on the Family. Also reprinted from John and Cindy Trent and Gary and Norma Smalley, *The Treasure Tree* (Dallas, TX: Word, 1992), 111–12.

11. Barbara Johnson, *Stick a Geranium in Your Hat and Be Happy* (Dallas, TX: Word, 1990), 107–8.

12. Adapted from Thomas A. Whiteman and Randy Petersen, "Becoming Your Own Best Friend," *Today's Christian Woman* (November/December 1984): 117–8.

13. Richard J. Foster, *Prayers from the Heart* (San Francisco: HarperSanFrancisco, 1994), 54.

Chapter Three

Growth: Sometimes I long to develop who I am

1. Dale Hanson Bourke, "What Motherhood Really Means," *Everyday Miracles* (Dallas, TX: Word Publishing, 1989): 2.

2. Ted Engstrom, *The Pursuit of Excellence* (Grand Rapids, MI: Zondervan, 1982), 17.

3. Gary Hardaway, "When Dreams Die," *Moody Monthly* (June 1986): 20.

4. Barbara Sher with Annie Gottlieb, *Wishcraft* (New York: Ballantine Books, 1979), 5.

5. Dottie McDowell, "Dottie's Delight Article," in Dave Ray, *Mom's Check-Up* (Royal Oak, MI: Core Ministries, 1994), 11.

6. Adapted from Cindy Tolliver, *At-Home Motherhood* (San Jose, CA: Resource Publications, 1994), 150–52.

7. Susan Solomon Yem, "Heading Home," *Virtue* (January/February 1995): 44.

8. John Trent, *Life Mapping* (Colorado Springs, CO: Focus on the Family, 1994), 7–8.

9. William J. Bennett, *The Book of Virtues* (New York: Simon & Schuster, 1993), 12.

10. Hellen Ferris, ed., *Favorite Poems Old and New* (Garden City, NY: Doubleday, 1957), 22.

11. Brenda Hunter, *What Every Mother Needs to Know* (Sisters, OR: Multnomah Press, 1993), 59.

Chapter Four

Intimacy: Sometimes I long to be understood

1. John Townsend, *Hiding from Love* (Colorado Springs, CO: NavPress, 1991), 34.

2. Heidi Brennan in Brenda Hunter, *In the Company of Women* (Sisters, OR: Questar, 1994), 25.

3. Brenda Hunter, *In the Company of Women* (Sisters, OR: Questar, 1994), 115–16.

4. Heidi Brennan in Brenda Hunter, *In the Company of Women* (Sisters, OR: Questar, 1994), 25.

5. Ibid., 26.

6. Joan Wulff, "Searching for Community in an Individualistic Age," *His Magazine* (March 1982): 1.

7. Richard Fowler, "The Intimacy Trap," *Discipleship Journal* 25 (1985): 12.

8. *Rocky Mountain News* (April 7, 1985).

9. Donna Partow, *No More Lone Ranger Moms* (Minneapolis, MN: Bethany House, 1995), 31.

10. Walter Wangerin, Jr., "You Are, You Are, You Are," *The Lutheran Journal* (January 24, 1990): 5.

11. Dale Hanson Bourke, *Everyday Miracles: What Motherhood Really Means* (Dallas TX: Word, 1989), 4.

12. Paul Tournier, *To Understand Each Other* (Atlanta, GA: John Knox Press, 1967), 29–30.

13. Cecil Osborne, *The Art of Understanding Your Mate* (Grand Rapids, MI: Zondervan, 1970), 159–60.

14. Elizabeth Cody Newenhuyse, "Friendship Fizzle," *Today's Christian Woman* (January/February, 1995): 51.

15. Reprinted and adapted from Cindy Tolliver, *At-Home Motherhood.* (San Jose, CA: Resource Publications, Inc., 1994), 40–41.

16. Marjorie Holmes, "Turning Sweet Nothings into Sweet Somethings," *Focus on the Family* (February 1988): 6.

17. Op. cit., Tolliver, 52–55.

18. Marsha Gallardo, "The Do's and Don'ts of Friendship Building," *Today's Christian Woman* (September/October 1994): 72.

19. Sister Basilea Schink, *The Hidden Treasure in Suffering* (Lakeland, MI: Marshall, Morgan, and Scott, 1985), 35–36.

Chapter Five

Instruction: Sometimes I don't know what to do

1. William Sears, M.D. and Martha Sears, R.N., *The Baby Planner* (Nashville, TN: Thomas Nelson, 1994), 2.

2. Beth Sharpton, "Who Will Be There for Us?" *Virtue* (June 1993): 44.

3. Susan L. Lenzkes, *When the Handwriting on the Wall Is in Brown Crayon* (Grand Rapids: Zondervan, 1981), 18.

4. Reprinted and adapted from Cindy Tolliver, *At-Home Motherhood.* (San Jose, CA: Resource Publications, Inc., 1994), 24–26.

5. From *Learning to Learn* by Gloria Frender, © 1990 by Incentive Publications, Inc., Nashville, TN 37215. Used by permission.

6. Adapted material by Eric Swanson for Campus Crusade for Christ (unpublished).

Chapter Six
Help: Sometimes I need to share the load

1. Donna Partow, *No More Lone Ranger Moms* (Minneapolis, MN: Bethany House, 1995), 13.

2. Ruth Barton, *Becoming a Woman of Strength* (Wheaton, IL: Harold Shaw, 1994), 193, 205.

3. Mary Stewart Van Leeuwen, *Gender and Grace* (Downers Grove, IL: InterVarsity Press, 1990), 157–58, 266.

4. Patricia Sprinkle, *Do I Have To?* (Grand Rapids, MI: Zondervan, 1993), 16.

5. Adapted from Gwen Ellis, *Thriving As a Working Woman* (Wheaton, IL: Tyndale House Publishers, 1995), 42–50.

6. Susan Yates, "And Then I Had Kids!" *Focus on the Family* (May 1990): 4.

7. Op. cit., Partow, 31.

8. Taken from Patricia Sprinkle, *Do I Have To?* (Copyright 1993 by Patricia Sprinkle. Used by permission of Zondervan Publishing House), 87.

9. Ibid., 106–7.

10. Ibid., 80.

11. Adapted from Dave Ray, *Mom's Check-Up* (Royal Oak, MI: Core Ministries, 1994), 52.

12. Ibid., 67.

Chapter Seven
Recreation: Sometimes I need a break

1. Dolores Curran, "Women and Fatigue," *Denver Catholic Register* (October 20, 1986).

2. Anne Morrow Lindbergh, *Gift from the Sea* (New York: Pantheon Books, 1955), 39.

3. Dr. Holly Atkinson in Dolores Curran, "Women and Fatigue," *Denver Catholic Register* (October 20, 1986).

4. Tim Hansel, *When I Relax, I Feel Guilty* (Elgin, IL: David C. Cook, 1979), 40.

5. Associated Press, "Study Finds Mother's Stress Affects Relations with Tots," *The Denver Post* (August 13, 1994).

6. Op. cit., Curran.

7. Denise Turner, "Keys to Happier Mothering," *Christian Herald* (May 1986), 23.

8. Grace Ketterman and Pat Holt, *When You Feel Like Screaming* (Wheaton, IL: Harold Shaw, 1988), 48.

9. William Arthur Ward, "Think It Over," *Fort Worth Star Telegram*.

10. Suzanne Britt Jordan, "Run, Oh Boy, Run!" *New York Times* (December 23, 1979).

11. Melanie McLean Michel, "Rock Around the Tot," *Aspire* (February/March 1995), 80–81.

12. Stacey C. York in Donna Partow, *No More Lone Ranger Moms* (Minneapolis, MN: Bethany House, 1995), 38.

13. Gordon Dahl, *Work, Play, and Worship in a Leisure-Oriented Society* (Minneapolis, MN: Augsberg, 1972), 12.

14. Richard Foster, *Celebration of Discipline* (San Francisco, CA: Harper & Row, 1978), 164.

15. Barbara Johnson, *Spatula Ministries Newsletter* (La Habra, CA: January, 1993).

16. H. Jackson Brown, Jr., *Life's Little Instruction Book* (Nashville, TN: Rutledge Hill Press, 1991).

17. Op. cit., Michel, 81.

18. Reprinted and adapted from Cindy Tolliver, *At-Home Motherhood* (San Jose, CA: Resource Publications, 1994), 178–80.

Chapter Eight

Perspective: Sometimes I lose my focus

1. Annie Dillard in Timothy K. Jones, "Death in the Mirror," *Christianity Today* (June 24, 1991): 31.

2. Dr. Marianne Neifert in Betty Johnson, "The Juggling Act of Dr. Mom," *Virtue* (March/April 1994): 39.

3. Charles R. Swindoll, *The Strong Family* (Grand Rapids, MI: Zondervan. 1991), 155.

4. Elizabeth Phillips Runkle, *Monmouth, the Key* (Fall 1994), 13.

5. Debbie Barr, *A Season at Home* (Grand Rapids, MI: Zondervan, 1993), 26.

6. Joy Jacobs, "Mysteries of Motherhood," *Christian Herald* (May 1986), 22.

7. Max Lucado, *God Came Near* (Portland, OR: Multnomah, 1987), 160.

8. Adapted from Barbara Johnson, *Mama, Get the Hammer: There's a Fly on Papa's Head* (Dallas, TX: Word, 1994), 42.

9. Taken from Bob Benson, *Laughter in the Walls* (Copyright 1969 by Impact Books. Used by permission of Zondervan Publishing House.).

10. Dr. Heartsill Wilson, "A New Day" (self-published).

Chapter Nine

Hope: Sometimes I wonder if there's more to life

1. Richard J. Foster, *Prayer: Finding the Heart's True Home* (Bloomington, MN: Garborg's, 1993), January 11.

2. Ibid., January 10.

3. Mayo Mathers, "What My Children Have Taught Me," *Today's Christian Woman* (November/December 1994), 90.

4. "The Search." Used by permission of Search Ministries, 5038 Dorsey Hall Dr., Ellicott City, MD 21042.

5. "Heart for the Harvest" (1991). Used by permission of Search Ministries, 5038 Dorsey Hall Dr., Ellicott City, MD 21042.

6. Excerpted from Pamela Reeve, *Faith Is . . .* (Portland, OR: Multnomah Books, 1970).

Look for these other great resources from MOPS International!

What Every Mom Needs Audio Pages

This condensed audio version of *What Every Mom Needs*, read by Elisa Morgan, reinforces the insights and encouragement from the book in a format to take on the go!

ISBN 0-310-20417-8

What Every Mom Needs Daybreak® perpetual calendar

You need encouragement all year long. So pick up this 365-day, full-color spiral calendar. Each day's reading contains insightful tidbits taken from *What Every Mom Needs*.

ISBN 0-310-96329-X

A Celebration of Motherhood audio program

This special audio tribute to mothers, portions of which were originally broadcast on Mother's Day 1995, contains 90 minutes of interviews and music, hosted by Elisa Morgan. Her guests include Gloria Gaither, Barbara Johnson, Rachael and Larry Crabb, Jan Dravecky, and others. Accompanying the interviews are songs written by Babbie Mason and Bonnie Knopf. The interviews and songs focus on the needs of mothers, as outlined in *What Every Mom Needs*.

ISBN 0-310-20416-X

Look for these great resources at your local Christian bookstore.

▙ ZondervanPublishingHouse

5300 Patterson Ave., S.E.
Grand Rapids, MI 49530